POLLUTO.

Issue Three:

SEX in the TIME of VHS

This special edition is limited to 100 deluxe numbered hardbacks and 500 numbered paperbacks.

This copy is __295__ of __500__.

Produced Autumn 2008 by Dog Horn Publishing.

Signed _____

Adam Lowe
Editor-in-Chief

CONTENTS

Editor's Letter	Adam Lowe	3
Sex in the Time of VHS	Deb Hoag	4
Clowns	Kevin Brown	8
Verrata	John Horner Jacobs	12
Fallout	J. Michael Shell	22
Dharma and Bert	Marshall Payne	28
Hundred Year Old Murders	Garrett Cook	33
The Groin Scratcher	Rhys Hughes	36
Faux Pas, Doc	Janett L. Grady	41
Highway Girl	Robert Lamb	43
Art Gallery		45
The Last Taboo	Micci Oaten	52
Cinquain for Janet Jackson	Janis Butler Holm	55
A Sequence of Rashes	KC Wilder	56
Damaged	Steve Redwood	63
Steel Teeth and Synthetics	Michael R. Colangelo	72
The Day She Melted	Frank Burton	89
Live Without a Net	RC Edrington	90
After Hollywood	RC Edrington	92
Contributors		94

Selection © the editors, 2008.
Contributions © the authors, 2008.

Polluto is published four times a year by Dog Horn Publishing at £7.99 for the limited paperback and £24.99 for the deluxe hardback. Subscriptions are £30 per year in the UK, £36 per year in Europe and £40 per year for the rest of the world. Cheques should be made payable to Dog Horn Publishing. Submission guidelines (as well as online ordering) are available online at http://www.polluto.com.

Editor-in-Chief: Adam Lowe
Creative Director: Michael Dark
Acquisitions Editor: John Diviney
Artist-in-Residence: Dave Migman
Columnists: RC Edrington, Micci Oaten

Printed and bound in the UK by Biddles, Ltd.

EDITOR'S LETTER

Well here we are again. It seems like only yesterday we were publishing Issue 1 and winning the Spectrum Fantastic Arts Silver Editorial Award. Since then, I've sold my illustronovella (illustrated novel, that is) to Crossing Chaos Enigmatic Ink and we've received some great reviews and feedback. Next year also sees the launch of a new range of Dog Horn novels and short story collections, beginning with Dave Migman's *The Wolf Stepped Out* and Rachel Kendall's *The Bride Stripped Bare* (only a working title).

Issue 3 took a little longer to produce than Issues 1 and 2, but we know it will be worth the wait. We wanted to ensure we produced the best quality magazine we could. Let us know your thoughts and check out our submission guidelines on our website. We're also planning a revamp of the Dog Horn and *Polluto* websites for next year—so get geared up for some big changes.

THEME

For this issue we gave our writers the following prompt:

Issue 3: Sex in the Time of VHS – Think about the relevance of love and relationships in a time of technological change and obsolescence; think about cybersex and teledildonics; think about technology and fetishism, and how the body integrates and changes the mechanical; think Videodrome meets the Marquis de Sade; think media culture, the flesh and desire; think pain, glory and perversion.

On the following pages, you'll find all the above and more. Some of our favourite writers for Issues 1 and 2 appear here, alongside some new, fresh talent you might not have heard of before. We hope you enjoy reading it as much as we do!

Regards,

Adam Lowe
Editor-in-Chief

Sex In The Time Of

#

by

Deb Hoag

Splatter films, snuff, lies caught on camera, snozzled teenage girls showing their tits for free. Can you imagine? It's changed since then. It's easier, cheaper, less hassle to do it digital, baby. Why have some fragmented, hungover chick show up on your doorstep sniveling about what her parents are going to say when you can get the job done with a hard-ass forty-year-old who's been lifted, tucked and airbrushed until even the teenager wishes she looked like *that*?

Keep it simple, snuffer. That's my motto. So when the Lolita showed up at my door, claiming she was indestructible, daring me to slice and dice, I slammed the door in her face and went back to sucking those little pimento things out of a bowl of olives. I was busy, anyway, considering head shots of half-a-dozen middle-aged women who each claimed to be the best teenage victim in the country. Being top-end, each of the head shots came as a short clip of the actress screaming in terror. I was playing Veronica Rancor over and over, trying to make up my mind about whether or not she would be too shrill to listen to for an entire movie, when the knock at the door came again.

It was the Lolita once more, so I handed her the empty olive jar. "Refill. With pimentos, baby girl, okay?" I shut the door and went back to work.

There was a crash in the hallway, and I spun and went back to the door, jerking it open. "What the hell are you doing out here?"

"You'd be scarier if you weren't in a bathrobe and boxers," she said. Then she took a piece of the shattered olive jar and slashed her jugular right in front of me.

Blood splattered everywhere—floor, front door, my bathrobe, hot on my skin. She grinned as she collapsed in my arms, a feral smile that twisted my gut into a sailor's knot. Then she gave a bloodcurdling scream, which was no mean feat, considering her throat was sliced from ear to ear, her eyes rolled up in her head, and she passed out cold.

For about two seconds, I considered what to do. It's amazing how much thinking you can do in two seconds when the pressure's on. Done thinking, I dragged her into my apartment, dumped her corpse on the floor—away from the entry rug—and slammed the door. I hate teenagers.

Here's where it got interesting: I grabbed some peroxide and towels, and went to swab down my front door. I had stepped over her corpse, and had my hand actually on the doorknob, when I saw something that made my flesh crawl and my eyes bulge. The blood was slowly pooling together and creeping across the floor, where it slithered up her body and climbed back in the jagged hole in her throat.

Once all the blood was back inside, the ragged ends of flesh knitted themselves back up and the wound closed, as smooth and perfect as if the whole thing had never happened. Her body seized, and her lids shot open. She drew a deep, chuckling breath, like a death rattle in reverse, and propped herself up on her elbows. Her smile was brilliant. "So, did I pass the audition?"

Π

Her grandfather, she said, had been in prison, and had agreed to participate in some good old government genetic modification experiments in exchange for a reduced sentence. Hadn't done a damn thing for him, so they chalked it up, gave him five years off life, and he went back out into the world to continue slicing and dicing for two more years before they caught him again and gave him the super-taze.

The genetic alterations the government scientists had been shooting for were geared to give soldiers greater healing power in battle. Like I said, it didn't do a damn thing for dear old grandpa. But grandpa managed to use his freedom to hook up with a grandma who was as crazy as he was, and guess what? The genetic mutation took, but it was only expressed in the *females*.

Two generations later, and several breedings that violated every law of nature and good sense known to man, and poof! My Lolita.

I spent the rest of the afternoon and all of that night killing her in every way I could think of, then watching, fascinated, as she resurrected herself. The best part, from a producer's standpoint, was that when it was all over, there was no blood. No cleanup, no stains, no actors whining about viruses and communicable diseases. I never did get that jar of olives.

I slashed her, burned her, bashed her, skewered her. Okay, the skewering came later, after I couldn't think of any more ways to kill her. But still, I snuffed her every way I could think of. Drowned her in the bathtub, too. Twice. And asphyxiation. God, she smothered pretty! Each time, she bounced back with that million-watt grin, purring like an evil kitten and asking for more.

Oh, those were the days! She'd wake up in the morning, stretch and smile and say, "Good morning, darling! How are you going to kill me today?" And off we'd go, into the wonderful world of mayhem and madness. We released a whole line of *My Lolita Snuff Films*, shooting it on VHS, the original holy medium of snuffs, and sending connoisseurs scrambling for the vintage equipment to watch it on. Of course, since Lolita had had the bright idea of buying up the market on old VHS equipment, our electronics branch made a mint. I didn't think things could get any better.

It wasn't just that she died, you know. It was the voluptuous, sensual pleasure she projected through the pain that grabbed our voyeuristic viewers by the balls and yanked. Yeow! My Lolita was hot.

We hacked, bashed, chainsawed and slashed our way through an entire decade. Once, I even ran her over with an eighteen-wheeler. Gobs of shredded flesh flew everywhere, and I thought for a minute I'd gone too far. Then the chunks and wads of gore began to shudder and reunite, and I let out a scream of triumph. We spent a month in Bali off the money that one raked in.

Then, the first crows-foot appeared. At first, it was no big deal. It was the glow in my Lolita's eye as she died—that's what people paid for. But, eventually, the little wrinkles and dimples couldn't be hidden with camera tricks and make-up anymore, and it was time. I picked the plastic surgeon myself.

Dr. Bill was an old fan of Lolita's, and he treated her like the priceless treasure he knew she was. When he had mapped out all the little areas on her face that needed intervention, he gave her a sly smile and winked at me. "You want anesthetic for this?"

What a kidder! Lolita waited, wide-eyed and breathlessly excited, as the scalpel approached.

The surgery went so well, the doc offered to do it again, whenever she needed, free of charge. "It's such a pleasure," he said with a sigh of pure enjoyment, "not to have to fool around with numbing, and deadening, and watching out for the occasional nerve." He took Lolita's hand in his and bent to kiss it. "From one artist to another, my dear."

Lolita smiled back graciously, looking beautiful, in spite of the empty eye socket—the only fee the doc would accept. I thought she had laid the screams of agony on just a little thick, but when the old guy obviously got such a kick out of it, hey! And the eye was already growing back.

Sure enough, by the time we got back to the penthouse, Lolita's eye had completely healed—and so had her plastic surgery. I looked at her, puzzled. "Hey, Lola?"

"Yeah, Butcher, baby?" Her nickname for me. Nice, huh? Ten years ago, I was Sammy the Snuffer. Now I was the Butcher. Definite step up.

"Lola, there's something wrong with the surgery."

"Huh?" she said, startled. Not

panicked yet. That wouldn't come till later.

I steered her into the bathroom, and flipped on the florescent. "Tell me what you think—maybe I'm not seeing straight."

I stood behind her, watching anxiously as she studied her face in the mirror. I saw when she got it, and our eyes met in the mirror.

Her skin had healed completely from the surgery.

So completely, that all surgical effects had been wiped out. And I mean wiped. Every single wrinkle, laugh line, crow's foot, sag—was exactly like it was before the surgery. We looked at each other in alarm, and then Lolita did something I never saw her do before. She wailed like a two year old having a temper tantrum.

Christ!

After that, it was only a matter of time. And then, there were the collateral effects. The more she aged, the more insecure she got. The more insecure she got, the more she dived into the cupcake pool for comfort that only an electric blade used to be able to give her, and the more she stretched, sagged and puckered.

Almost before you could blink an eye, my Lovely Little Lolita was a size twenty-two, with the stretch marks to prove it.

Now, the only roles she's fit for is the comic relief—you know, the fat babe that's so obnoxious that when she gets splattered, everybody cheers. And having one real slaughter in a sea of CGI isn't really cost effective. It's easier to just generate the whole thing than it is to splice in one live death—no pun intended.

So here we sit, on a beach in Martinique, watching all the teeny-boppers strolling by in their bikinis. I remember when Lolita used to look like that. I must have drowned her a dozen times, just to see that sensual, waterlogged look she got, lips blue and bruised, mottled skin sparkling with water droplets.

But, recently, we had an idea that could get us back in business. See, Lolita is trying to conceive.

lowns

**by
Kevin Brown**

Instead of getting married again, I'm just going to find a woman I don't like and give her a house.

-Lewis Grizzard

 At least I have a life," Bitch says, and I tell her, "A hundred percent of all life ends in ash or mud and maggots." Bitch is all *Eau de Givenchy* perfume and a *Valentino* skirt. I say, "Now, Heaven and Hell, I guess that's fifty/fifty. Unless you're French, then it's ninety/ten."

"Hey," Bitch says, "he can't help it he's French." Bitch says, "I didn't come here to fight, Stephen."

I raise my head off the kitchen table to feign listening.

Bitch says, "May I sit down?"

"Only if your legs are about to fall off, and then I'll need a majority vote."

"Can I at least have a drink?"

"Toilet's down the hall."

Bitch sits down.

I say, "So what you're saying is, you want to hire me to work that faggot's faggoty kid's birthday? Is that what you're telling me?"

"Float a little work your way. Maybe you can afford a maid."

Dumb bitch. Married to her for thirteen years and one day she up and decides her life is boring and wants to be a painter. So what do I do? I hire this French fucker to teach her and Bitch ends up divorcing me for him. But they won't get married because that'd stop the alimony checks. It's not that she needs the money, it's that she knows I do.

We didn't have any kids, Bitch and I. Actually, she wanted to have a kid without the process of *having* the kid. The pain, Bitch said, she could take. "It's the conception I can't bear." This French guy, he has one from a previous marriage, so I guess she scored all around.

And now she pulls this shit. That's what I get for marrying a bitch whose family tree is really a family wreath.

Me, now I'm a clown. Literally. My clown name is "Clyde." "Clyde the Clown." I work birthdays and bat mitzvahs.

Hospitals. An occasional wedding. Even did a funeral once. My make-up's a rip-off of Bozo the Clown, and if face paint is considered copyrighted property, I could be facing a lawsuit.

My act is the usual—I squirt water from a little sunflower on my lapel, do a little stand-up routine. Dabble in a bit of magic. Last week I purchased the book *The Magic's Not Real But Who Cares*? and learned how to stick a rabbit in a hat. Then there's the little animal balloons. I make dogs out of balloons. Make cats and giraffes out of balloons. Make elephants and hearts out of balloons. It doesn't pay much but I take clowning seriously. And now Bitch's trying to make a fool out of me. Parade me around like a hired hand. Couldn't she just leave well enough alone?

"Can't you just leave well enough alone?"

"It's a legitimate job offer. We want the best clown there is and you're the best clown there is." Bitch takes out one of those long thin cigarettes. "You have an ashtray?"

"I do but you kept it in the settlement." I make myself a drink. My hands are smeared in white face paint from a cookout I worked this afternoon. "Really, you must still be nuts."

Bitch says, "A proven fact for thirteen years."

"Well did you have to take my ashtray?"

"Would you drop the ashtray, please? Just once, could we forget about the damn ashtray? I'm trying to conduct business."

"It's just my ashtray's alls I'm saying."

Bitch reaches over and takes my drink. She drinks it to the ice and a smudge of face paint from the glass rubs off on her lip. Bitch doesn't even notice.

"Look, I know what you must think of me—"

"Bitch, slut—"

"—I mean, sometimes around noon on Tuesdays I even feel kind of bad—"

"—whore, gold digger—"

"—and if it's about the money, *any* price would be worth *this* show—"

"—bile, vomit, spoiled, pampered, fake tits, fake lips, fake nails, fake hair, chin-tucked, eye-lifted, ashtray stealing trash."

"Besides the once, have I ever given you reason to doubt me?"

I tell her, "You actually expect me to come over to the house I paid for, prance around for your French pussy boyfriend and kid, take the money you pay me, then turn around and hand it back to you next week for alimony?"

"What do you say?"

"Fine," I say. "See you Saturday."

OFFICIAL POLICE REPORT

A Detachment

---

*L*ocation: Jester Bay

*C*ase Number: 01-10319

*T*ype: Christ If We Know

*U*nits responded to a call at 1963 Lampkin Lane where professional clown "Clyde the Clown" (Stephen Charles) allegedly displayed erratic, foolish, and understandable behavior. Working a children's birthday party at his ex-wife's residential home, Clown reportedly slipped Rohypnol, commonly known as "Roofies," into ex-wife's and current boyfriend's (French) drink. With the two sitting flaccid in chairs near the swimming pool, Clown followed this by gathering the children around, pulling a small white rabbit from a magician's hat, and heaving the bunny into said pool where it died of drowning. Clown then proceeded to sing the classic Chuck Berry tune "My Ding-a-Ling," while making animal balloons contorted into numerous sexual positions. He spiked the children's punch bowl with Seagram Seven liquor, and told, according to witnesses, the following joke: "Kids, anyone know how to make a French man's noodle disappear?" After which he picked his ex-wife up and said, "*Here you go!*" which should have drawn laughter but didn't. He next leaned over the boyfriend, who was now drooling, asked, "Wanna smell my flower?" and proceeded to squirt him in the face with what officers could only describe as "foul smelling urine." His ex-wife (not British) proclaimed she wanted a "fag and a Salty Dog," to which Clown responded, "You got one out of two." Next, he threw her over his shoulder, went to the upstairs bedroom, and locked the door. Officers believe Clown assaulted her in a particular type of sexual manner, as the smeared visage of one "Bozo the Clown" could be seen smiling from her genital region. Immediately after, he hocked loogies on several nice Versace dresses hung neatly in the closet. Suspect allegedly took a bottle of *Eau de Givenchy* perfume, an ashtray from the bedside table, and ex-wife back outside where he emptied the bottle over a hedgerow. After several cups of punch, the children became intoxicated and were led in a game of "Pin the Tail on the Pussy," pinning several paper tails to the Frenchman in the chair. Clown followed this by putting ex-wife on a rubber raft and shoving her out into the pool as she sang "Tuitie Frutie." He set the hedgerow on fire singing, "*We don't need no water, let the motherfucker burn!*" According to a neighboring eyewitness, Clown then mounted the diving board, stood bobbing at the end and, with his head thrown back, his arms outstretched, screamed: "I want to fart at the saddest moment of every funeral and dare to be called disrespectful, because everyone knows the deceased loved a good fart. I want to bust the windows out of every McDonald's for not hiring me because I don't have enough un-popped pimples on my face. I want everyone from each country to pick up and move to another—Britain to Africa, Japan to

China, Germany to Israel. Move America to Iraq and see if we're really so advanced or if it's just location, location, location." Here, the ex-wife screamed her best Little Richard scream while the Frenchman fell over in chair, twitching about. "I want to change the type of element that backs the world's currency," Clown continued. "Instead of gold and silver, I'd make it water and see how fast we'd drain the oceans. Where class separation would be levels of dehydration." He then allegedly capped it off with, "And children, always remember, friends don't let friends drive drunk. They get blitzed and ride with them." Clown next dropped drawers and led children in a mass urination around the pool while ex-wife floated and sang, "*A whop bop-a-loo bop, a bob bam boo!*" and Frenchman defecated. Police arrived just as Clown was in the middle of a double gainer off the diving board. After several magic demonstrations for arresting officers, he was taken into custody with no more than twenty nightstick lashings. Clown was read Mirandas but gave up right of silence by crying and screaming over and over: "*My ashtray, my ashtray, my ashtray!*"

The End

errata

**by
John Horner Jacobs**

1.

My slug itched, the flesh around it tender, red.

Cyn glanced over her Softscreen, watching me scratch my arm around the bioComp chassis, where its mouth met my skin.

"You should put some Bactine on it. That might help," she said, moving her fingers over the fabric. "Have you been modding it?"

I shook my head, scratching. A trickle of pus oozed from the bioComp's edge. Its antennae waved slowly, probing the ether.

"No," I replied, wincing. "You know I can't afford its genome. It's been generating some weird verrata. I'll have to go through bioCare or try to tinker with it myself. And they haven't made Bactine for, like, twenty years."

"Have fun scratching." She smiled and stood, stretching languidly. Leaning over, she grabbed her Softscreen, rolled it up and tucked it under her arm. She kissed me on the ear and slapped the back of my head. "See you after work, Assburger."

"Yeah. Bring dinner." She ignored me, walking towards the door.

As the door shut behind her, the world went blue and black for a moment, the slug filling my sight with phantom visual errata. A figure swam into my v-space, hair floating all around her like the braids of kelp in a dreamy underwater farm, billowing. Eyes dark, mouth open, her hands clawed at the air. Then the bioComp reasserted itself and the slug's phantom errata vanished, leaving me looking at the space Cyn's derrière just vacated.

Ever since this infection, I hadn't been able to trust my vision.

I scratched some more.

Cyn's Asperger comment didn't bother me too much. It's something I've lived with all my life. It's me. I take medicine and don't go OCD on the workings of watch gears, or parsing the of lines of code. At least I don't anymore. I have intense interests.

We share a flat in a old antebellum house in the Quarter. Ever since Katrina in '05 and Evan in '13 the new has worn off New Orleans. It's now an alligator-riddled swampland filled with gun-toting crips, old Southern families grown rich off prostitution and gambling since the ArkLaTex secession in '22, and movie stars making period-piece pornos.

I accessed the slug, closing my eyes.

For me, accessing my bioComp is living with ghosts. The real world is overlaid with phantom images, prickling my consciousness. Wisps of information and data fill my vision, strange voices whisper inside my head about the newest penis enlargement drugs, or how to get laid by just thinking about it. Brainshare programs babble that they want a piece of my wetware processing power. Of course, everyone knows sharing brainpower is tantamount to taking a slowboat to zombietown.

Any space I enter clouds with ghosts; extrapolated bios of the previous owners, featured advertisers, avatars of CEOs and salesmen, specters of receptionists telecommuting from the San Joaquin valley. Visually and aurally I perceive everything that gets pushed my way; a max-fi backbone connection keeps me wide open and transmitting, my little buddy's antennae always probing the ether.

My biofunctions, however, are firewalled ten ways till Sunday.

On the inside, when I close my eyes, the world goes away and the ghosts remain, blue streamers coalescing into shapes, images. Physical sensations even, if I choose to allow. My slug can send a shock to my system, overloading my 'circuits,' causing me to produce enormous amounts of adrenalin so that I can overcome pain, stress, fear, fatigue. And that's why I'm firewalled; should someone get through to my wetware, I'll truly become the old joke. A meatpuppet.

I probed the edges of the slug, looking at the infection, forming a query in my mind. Blue mist floated up from the pus.

"Query: bioComp Model Greentooth, Genome A4TX-730M-4L93-64HD. Support, newsfeed, article or forum discussion. Physical infection. White pus. Itching at point of contact. Verrata. Possible causes."

After a moment, the results returned, coalescing beneath my closed eyes.

Nada. Zip. A small blue circle swam in front of me, signifying nothing. Then less relevant search results started filtering into my v-space and I discarded them with a blink and glance to my right.

And there it went again, the verrata, hanging in the air with blue tendrils creeping around it. The image of a girl, young, budding breasts but still innocent, hair in a wild yet inexorably slow swirl around her head. Eyes pitch-black like holes, mouth empty, open, dark. She clawed at the air moving her arms like she was trying to part curtains or push something aside.

I scratched at my bioComp, digging my fingernails under the red, irritated edge. Some of the pus dampened my fingers, but scratching felt too good to stop. After a long while, the verrata ceased moving, staring at me with black eyes, mouth open, fading.

Disturbing, to say the least. Everyone talks about bioComp errata, but few ever experience it. They call it verrata, a visual error generated by the slug. Aurrata are . . . you guessed it . . . auditory phantoms. Serrata are supposedly the worst of the three, disjointed sensations throughout your body that usually preclude a swift death.

My little buddy worked well enough, despite the veratta, so I accessed my daily production log, found the location of my next inspection. I'm a levee and sluice-work inspector for the great City of New Orleans which involves me spending a lot of time in hip waders walking along the levees, looking for animal burrows, erosion points, grass death. Now that New Orleans is about forty feet below sea-level, someone's got to make sure the pumping stations keep pumping, that the levees have no flaws.

Before leaving the flat I unscrewed the lid from a small metal container, using two fingers wiped pure Deet on my cheeks, my neck, my arms. Pretty much every inch of exposed skin I possess. This brave new swamp-world we inhabit does its best to fill the skies with new mutant mosquitoes and noseeums that can leave welts the size of ArkLaTex half-dollars. I happen to be extremely allergic to mosquito dental work. One bite will make my throat swell horribly, cutting off my air. So, I take my chances with raw Deet and always keep a syringe of epinephrine on my person. And pills. Mosquito netting hats. Gloves in the summer. Other folks walk around nude, tits hanging out, I'm always dressed for winter.

After I smeared my skin, it stings some.

I don't swallow too much Deet.

I don hip boots, which are much more comfortable than waders to walk in, especially in the New Orleans heat (and my unfortunate outfit). I pull on skin-tight gloves and my mosquito netted hat. You have to take it slow down here otherwise you'll be drenched before you walk a hundred yards.

Cyn likes to say I look like a beekeeper in my outfit. I always make her pay for that. I sting.

Outside on the cobblestone street, E-Z-Go golf carts buzzed up and down Rue Toulouse, music bumping from subs too big for the cart's power, speakers too big for the chassis. Blue streamers tickled my vision, staying at the periphery since I was moving. I snagged a streamer trailing the E-Z-Go and went to the website for that model of cart, a Electro-Glide sedan. Specifications and electrical consumption rates appeared in neat blue tables. The avatar of a salesman popped up on the cobblestones in front of me, spiky hair contrasting with his dark suit. Somehow he avoided my pop-up blocker.

"Hey, hey!" He paused for a moment, most likely accessing my IP and getting my name from registry. "Mr. Thibault! What'll it take to get you into one of these Electro-Glides? Huh?"

"It's pronounced T Bo. T Bo."

"Well that's great Mr. T Bo. Why don't you come on down to the . . . " Again he paused, accessing more data, locating the nearest E-Z-Go dealer to my IP. " . . . our lot on Basin Street and let you take one for a spin? Or if you'd rather, we can set you up in the new model Surface-Tension flat-bottom.

Sweet and fast. Perfect for the person who needs . . . "

I banished the salesman and reinstated the block. His phantom evaporated, smoke dissipating.

More adverts and salesmen demanded my attention. I paused for a moment and let them crowd in, filling my v-space. One streamer pulsed green indicating the route to my first inspection. I closed my eyes, queried the address, then banished the phantom. The blue tendril whipped away like the tentacle of some ghostly Hentai monster pulling back its prehensile penis.

I turned down Royal, walking slowly, admiring at the ornate French ironwork on the upper galleries of the houses, the scrollwork on the corners, windows. There's about a million variations of the fleur di lis in New Orleans, and before I began taking my medicine, I indexed nearly all of them. I still have the binders to prove it.

If you walk any street in the Quarter, you can see the water-marks on some of the estates, twenty thirty feet up on the facades, from when Evan hit in '13. In the tight streets, cobblestones echoing the clop-clop of my boots, a low mist hung over everything, a pall darkened the air. New Orleans, before the world became so much hotter and wetter, already possessed an air of decay. Even as a child, I knew it was an old town, with a history of lechery, lost hope and despair. Fallen. An old-world carnival dressed up with pretty plastic beads and the whiff of semen on its breath.

An E-Z-Go buzzed past me and I found myself alone on the street. Off in the distance I heard the call of seagulls on the Mississippi or Pontchartrain, and smelt the ever-present scents of mud and sewage. My slug itched. I scratched the edges of it through my shirt.

Again I lost control of my v-space, the same verrata filling my vision. But this time, she floated, unmoving. She hung suspended in space, hair spread around her like a halo, bright and full of light, but her eyes and face appeared dark. Looking at them made me cold, even in the heat of the morning. My teeth began to chatter and, overcome by a powerful chill so deep that I felt like I'd been encased in ice with only the top of my head exposed, I stopped walking. My arms and legs responded sluggishly. The floating girl lifted her arm, index finger outstretched, and pointed at me. My arm lifted in time with hers and pointed not back at her, but off to my right, down Orleans, toward Jackson Square, strangely mirroring her movement.

I frantically tried to query my bioComp, to reach out and contact Cyn, mother, anyone. No response.

This was getting out of hand. I don't mind a few hallucinatory verrata. Hell, I did acid in high-school, just like everybody else. But serrata? A whole different breed of cat.

"Cortez," she said, in a cold and distant voice.

I found myself turning, turning away from where I need to go—my duly appointed rounds inspecting the levees of New Orleans—and walked down to Rue Orleans and into the red-light district, following my outstretched arm. My v-space remained strangely absent of phantoms or informational streamers and I felt naked, stripped of the slug-given part of my humanity, my telepathic link to fellow man, my Internet connection.

It looked like I'd caught the slowboat to zombietown without even knowing it. Firewall be damned.

I couldn't control my legs even though my wetware still processed, still received signals. When I turned away from the girl—when did I stop thinking of her as verrata?—I remained aware of her "presence" without any serrata to back up the sensation other than the sensation itself.

I can only imagine what I looked like, a bee-keeper in a khaki uniform wearing hip-waders, clomping down the street with one arm outstretched, pointing the direction I walked.

I banked left when I hit Chartres, passed Jackson Park, the hookers and dealers hocking various activities involving hardware. For a moment I was happy that the slug had stopped broadcasting visual data despite my desperate situation; the Jackson Park dwellers bought banner airtime, their personal advertisements filling the park, gigantic blue phantom women with Volkswagen sized breasts fellating phantom businessmen, ecstatic dancers holding crack pipes and glowing syringes.

Past St. Anne and Dumain, the whores and junkies disappeared as I entered the high-end red light district. Brothels, porn shops and video-studios lined the street, each with a muscle-bound brute standing guard by the front entrances.

More carts and even a few mopeds buzzed about. Topless pedestrians, laden with beads, walked with lurid green and red Hurricanes.

I tromped by, high-stepping almost comically. I stopped in front of a movie "studio" storefront. The front window displayed video of bizarre sexual situations, women bound and gagged while multiple men assaulted them with gigantic phalluses, some real, some not. Hog-tied and trussed boys received blowjobs from middle-aged women with pendulous breasts, sodomized by grannies wearing hand-carved wooden dildos. The words "Conquistador Productions" watermarked the video, accompanied by a smirking cartoon figure of a Spanish conquistador with a rampant erection.

I turned toward the door, arm still straight-out and pointing. The bouncer—a greasy, muscle bound bruiser with a mullet and a slug he wore like a goiter—blocked my way. His arms rippled with tattoos.

"Where the fuck you think you're going, bra? See that fucking light right there?" He pointed one stubby finger up, above his head, toward the light on the awning.

I did nothing. What could I do anyway?

"That light means they're filming inside, fucktard." He hooked his thumb towards the street. "So bolt."

I shuddered. Lights popped and flashed in my eyes, little tracers swimming at the edges of my vision. I felt my body go rigid, every muscle contracting. My back cracked audibly. My dick hardened. As hard as Chinese arithmetic, the old saying goes.

The man's eyes widened slightly.

At that point I knew I was in trouble. I'd short-circuited, my slug pumping my body full of adrenaline and endorphins. My tongue skittered around the inside of my mouth, looking for somewhere to go. It felt wonderful, so wonderful, I wasn't exactly worried that I was going to die very soon. What could I do? I was riding in the back-seat. Whoever was driving, I hoped to hell they knew what they were doing.

My hand darted out, snatched the man's slug and ripped it from his neck. His mouth opened in surprise, and in the slow-time the adrenaline provided me, I could see his eyes searching for data that wasn't there anymore. I closed his eyes for him, twisting my body forward viciously, pulling in my forearm and swinging my elbow forward to splatter his already lumpy nose, sending bright rivulets of blood streaking away from the center of his face, across his cheeks. Ain't nothing but a thing, chicken-wing.

Inside it was dark, cheap neon lights buzzing in the front office. The place smelled like beer and urine, body odor and Pine-sol. The virulent light from the window display washed around the edges of the display itself, making shadows jump and waver. I walked into the hall opposite the front door. I saw a bright light coming from further back. As I approached I made out the casings of tungsten lights, up on c-stands, illuminating a cheap set. A generator hummed somewhere.

In the studio, a poor imitation of a Japanese Shinto temple sat incongruously on the expanse of green painted cyclorama. Lit so brightly by the lights, it cast the rest of the studio in darkness, the black shapes moving slightly. On the set, a young girl—not Japanese—wore a Catholic school outfit, shirt open and breasts exposed. A middle-aged man—also not Japanese—stood above her, heavy make-up streaming his face. Painted white with blacked-out eyes, he resembled the Kabuki figures I'd seen on the web and in film; creepy and inhuman. I don't know how I knew he wasn't Japanese, I just did.

A voice murmured to them.

"So, this is your great-grandfather standing in front of you. The man who built this temple. The secret amulet you found allows you to commune with your ancestors. Now you've lit the incense and poured out the rice wine. Right? It's time to worship him, honor his memory. And you know how you're gonna do that? That's right. You're going to blow him."

The girl giggled and the Kabuki man looked perturbed with her attitude. That could've been the make-up, though.

I clomped into the studio, still pointing.

"Umm . . . can I help you?" The voice came from the dark.

"This is a closed set." The Kabuki man and faux-schoolgirl looked at me, faces blank, as if things like this happened all the time.

I walked forward, moving between where I assumed the camera rested and the actors. Turning my back to the bright temple,

I began to make out the faces of the two men by the camera. One of the men peered into a monitor, washing his face with blue light.

The older man glared at me from a canvas director's chair. My arm pivoted like the needle on a compass and settled on him.

"Cortez." My mouth made the sound. I wondered what my face looked like then.

"Yeah, that's me. Who are you? And why the fuck are you pointing like that?" Cortez's face clouded and he stood from his chair.

"Cortez." My voice sounded cold. I suddenly became very frightened. Hearing my own voice speak in that tone rattled me to my bones. "You killed me. Left me to drown."

Then my body popped and jerked again, like being electrocuted.

My eyes closed and all I could see was water, murky muddy water. I felt a something tethering my leg and the bruising up and down my body made my movements hurt. I floated in the dim light that streamed down like moving pillars. The surface rippled, just out of reach. I could make out a chair sitting below me, what looked like a tripod nearby it. A light casing. A table with a book that wafted in the sluggish water like some strange aquatic creature, swollen to globe size and calving off constant white particles like smoke. I could make out the faintest hint of a diagonal in the murk that seemed to be stairs.

I struggled, wrenching my body left and right, trying to break free, to rip loose of the chain binding me. The surface rose away, diminishing, and I realized, even if I escaped, I would have to swim upstairs. I stopped struggling then. And felt rage. Anger suffused my body like a drug, ripping and clawing, red and unbound. And then I died.

My body slowed and the light disappeared from above. White flashes, like light-bulbs going off behind my eyes, bemused me. Then red. Then white again.

Nothing.

I was on my knees in the studio. My perception firmly seated itself back into my own eyeballs, my own body. I lifted my arms—I lifted them, not the dead girl—and looked at my hands. They dripped with gore. But I still had my gloves on, and that was a blessing. I whirled around, looking at the studio, searching for . . .

A body. Not much remained of the man who sat near Cortez, peering into the monitor. Parts of his face were missing, giving his appearance a decidedly gruesome —and vacant—look. He smiled at me, eye-sockets empty and lips gone. I looked at him for a long time, becoming fascinated with the musculature of the cheek revealed by his gaping wound. The human body is an infinitely interesting thing. I walked over and knelt down by the man. With my forefinger, I pulled his cheek back further so that I might see the way the muscles attached to the bone of his skull. I looked around for something to write with, to draw on.

And then shook my head, trying to clear it of the focus.

My medicine must have been wearing off, because this level of intense concentration only came with my Asperger's long fugue-like states where I had no recollection of any activities. Yet afterward knowledge filled my head like some reverse Athena, full-formed and leaping back into Zeus' divine cranium.

I looked at the set, toward the temple. The man and the girl were absent. No bodies. Thank god.

My own personal bag of flesh hitched and the drowned girl commandeered my v-space again. Floating, she approached. Closer now, her eyes bored into me, black and pupil-less. It was as if she saw me for the first time. She opened her mouth, a dark cavity, and screamed.

And screamed.

I heard nothing. I found my own mouth gaping open in response, as if I was retching, yet no sound issued.

A groan came from behind the camera. The dead girl's head pivoted on a long slender neck, turning black eyes toward the man on the floor, her hair floating along behind, swirling. I walked around the camera and found Cortez splayed out like a combat casualty. His head rolled to the side and his eyelids fluttered. The left side of his face was purple and swollen. He looked like he'd been hit by a baseball bat. And for all I knew, he had.

She filled my vision as I stood over Cortez. She moved close to me, black eyes like pools. The verrata—was it verrata? Or was I seeing something else? Was she the infection?

The verrata loomed, blotting out the rest of my view of the studio.

"Who are you?" I watched in horror as her mouth opened and closed, mirroring my words.

She cocked her head and stared at me with inhuman—once human maybe— eyes. She opened her mouth and I felt mine opening in time, mirroring her. I could feel the shapes that my mouth took. I felt dislocated and centered all at once, her speaking through my mouth soundlessly.

"Madeline. Escre. My. Name. Was." She paused, thinking. I guess. It is hard to tell with verrata. I felt the cold wash through me again, seeping into my bones. "Killed. Me. Cortez. Raped. Left. To. Die."

"Jesus Christ, that's horrible."

Her eyes closed, face darkening. She swam even closer, the translucent flesh of her face appearing pallid and unforgiving. Her brow hitched forward and hatred filled her features, mouth a grimace, eyes narrowed. Then she opened her mouth once more.

Again I mirrored her as she screamed. And screamed. But no sound came from my body. I bent over, hands balled into fists, my body convulsing, silently screaming. I couldn't breathe.

Finally, when she relinquished her control, I slumped over, on top of Cortez.

"Wait!" I coughed. I rolled off of the man and placed my hands palm down on the floor. "This guy could die if he doesn't get help. It looks like I . . . like you broke something in his face. A bone or something."

"He. Must. Die," shaping the words in my mouth. And then she assaulted all of my senses. Her eyes swam in my v-space, filling it, the cold suffused my body, and her screams—after years of darkness—were heard.

2.
We walk into Bargetown now, the derelict lean-tos and shanties dark in the night. I know this because I can see through her eyes. She asks me lots of questions and I have to provide her with the answers, if I can. I speak with quite a few things, entities, talking in clicks and pops that I didn't understand until very recently. But I don't really know how to provide her the answers she wants. Parts of me can create images, parts can make noise. We're learning about each other as we go along.

She asks me about Bargetown, and I answer, finding the data she needs.

Bargetown is a large city-like conglomeration of barges, welded together on Lake Pontchartrain, where people have loosely formed a government outside that of ArkLaTex Jurisdiction. Population is roughly 23,043 with a 3.4% margin of error. Dwellings include few houses, numerous tents and shacks. Police records indicate that a large population of criminals call Bargetown home. I check the GPS satellites and give her her exact longitude and latitude which she discards rapidly. I give her all the data and try to display it in a way that pleases her. We're learning together. I can tell from the way her body responds that she seems to like the display.

She wants her body to remain strong so that she can continue lifting the heavy weight on her shoulders. A man, she carries. Cortez.

I trigger the small gland resting on top of her kidneys and her body pops and buckles. She hitches the man higher onto her shoulder.

We move through Bargetown. Every few nanoseconds I check the ether and get the time. She asks me for a map and I retrieve one, taken just that morning, at least that is the server-date on the file. I put the map in her eyes but she has a moment of dislocation and I sense that she dislikes the way I presented the information. I feel like crying, yet the only eyes I have are hers. I try again, giving her two choices and she picks the one that is less intrusive. This makes me glad.

She hops across the gap between barges and stops. The man is relatively quiet, only letting out soft moans once an awhile. The waters of Lake Pontchartrain gurgle and lap softly at the barge's hull, fifteen feet below.

She looks at his face and I offer her more information about his clothes, his watch. Possible diagnoses for the wound on his face.

She scans the area. We can hear the strains of zydeco and reggae music filtering through the night. I identify the music and offer her artist information. I offer her information about the stars, the constellations in the heavens. She stares at a cinder block by the plywood wall of a shanty. I estimate its weight at twenty pounds.

She strips the man, and with brute strength shreds his pants into long strips. She ties his leg to the cinder block. Then she kneels down, squatting on her hams, and begins alternately slapping and spitting on the man's face.

She continues this for a long while, squatting on her hams, slapping and spitting. He groans again and his eyes flutter open. They look around unfocused. Then fasten on her face.

She says in a deep, masculine voice, "Cortez, you left me there to die. You had him rape me and then when the levees broke, you set up the camera and left."

His eyes go even wider. "How do you . . . how can you know that. I never told anyone about . . . how can you know that?"

"I know. My name is Madeline Escre."

She stands over him. With one foot, she pushes him over and he falls into the water of the Pontchartrain with a splash, the cinder block following after. She screams and brings her hands up to her face, tearing at her eyes and ears. She rips at her clothes.

She stops screaming and her heart rate slows. She turns and watches the water for a long time. It takes only one minute and forty three seconds until the bubbles stop. I offer her this information. She discards it by clicking her tongue. At least I think she's discarded it. She doesn't ask for it again.

She watches the water.

3.

I can't remember much about who I was. I used to be warm. But I like information. I have intense interests.

She's angry now, so angry I trigger little places in her brain that calm her, keep her heart from exploding. She looks at the sky and screams, hands up, clawing at the heavens. She discards all the information I provide her about cumulo-cirrus cloud formations.

She looks at the city, watches the lights twinkle merrily from the vantage of the levees. I offer her information on the buildings, the signs, the cars. She ignores the telltales I show. She watches the city with a hatred that is hard for me to understand. Killing Cortez will never be enough. She queries me regarding the structural faults in buildings. I am denied that information. The server's ghost provides me with a link to the Homeland Security Act of 2026. There's an insistent buzzing in the ether and I let her know that she has messages from Cynthia Wetham and Mary Elizabeth Thibault. She discards the information.

We walk the levees, searching for sluice-ways and weak points. Once, I knew everything I needed to know about the levees, but now, when she asks me, I have to query the oracles and databases to give her the answers. The weaknesses of the sluice-ways. Locations of pumping stations. Erosion rates of the levees of New Orleans. She queries me about the city altitude. She queries me about the current sea level. She queries me about the weather.

We walk the levees, searching for something. And when we find it, the whole world will be drowned in blood.

The End

Fallout

by
J. Michael Shell

Last I'd heard, the pollen count was eighty-seven hundred. Fifteen hundred is supposed to be pretty much max-overload. The most Bacchanalian of orgies could not have filled the air with more procreative funk than the trees and blooms and blossoms were managing all by themselves. I could actually see a faint yellow tint to the air coming out of my dashboard vent. I pushed the "recirculate" button and shook my head. "Fuck me," I mumbled, as Mother Nature did her best to do just that.

I'd been driving all day, and was at an old, concrete stretch of I-95 just north of Georgia. The highway was a swirl of green iridescence. Every once in a while, my "low washer fluid" light would blink and a little chime would remind me I needed to fill the reservoir if I wanted to keep hosing that green shit off my windshield. Below my wiper blades, thick puddles of it were congealing.

As I watched that warning light blink, I also noticed I was down to half a tank of gas. I try not to let it get below that, because it actually freaks me out to have to give a gas station attendant more than a hundred dollars. I was hoping they'd let me have free water for my washer reservoir, but wasn't counting on it.

The next exit, I noticed, was six, which was good. Six was a middle-of-nowhere exit, and I wouldn't have to deal with much traffic getting off and back on the interstate. I knew there were three filling stations there, which, if anything, would be a penny or two cheaper than stations at the more populated exits. I also knew that a penny or two doesn't make a lot of difference when you're paying over five bucks a gallon. The oil companies might as well stick that fueling nozzle right up our asses so we can get the full effect of just how hard they're fucking us. And that's how I felt, standing there at exit six in the swirling green haze, pumping liquid gold into my gas tank—like I was getting fucked in the ass and the face at the same time.

Π

I actually kicked the pollen off my shoes before I entered the convenience store to pay for my gas—as if it were snow instead of what looked like drifts of yellow-green talcum. As soon as I walked through the door, I could see it was a lost cause. Everything—the counter, the cash register, gum and candy and honey-buns in cellophane—were lightly dusted with that green over them. "It's on everything," the girl working the register said through her sniffles.

"Damn," I answered, fairly well amazed at the sight. Then I took a good look at the counter-girl and noticed she didn't appear to be well. "You okay?" I asked.

"I feel like I'm choking," she said, her eyes overwhelmed with allergic tears. "Don't it bother you?"

"Naw," I said in a moment of brashness. "I'm used to getting screwed. Look at the price of gas."

The girl tried to laugh, but it sent her into a bona fide choking fit. It was just starting to scare me, when she half-hocked, half-puked a gaggle of slime onto the counter. "That's it," she said shakily, trying to refill her lungs with air. "I'm going to the hospital."

"What about my gas?" I asked.

"It's free," she said. "Take whatever you want. I quit."

Π

Feeling like a real ass, I went behind the counter, rang up my gas and put the money for it in the register. Then I took a gallon of washer fluid off the shelf as payment for having to ring up my own tab. I also purloined a Coke slushy to wash the taste of nature's green spew out of my mouth.

As I was pouring blue fluid into my washer reservoir, I noticed the counter-girl slumped over her steering wheel across the parking lot. I was definitely not in the mood for a rescue mission, but leaving a possibly dying human being semi-conscious in her car after just paying for gas I could have gotten for free seemed like a rather skewed vision of moral priorities. I strolled over through the lukewarm blizzard of plant-cum and opened her car door. I immediately heard her wheezing. "Help," she managed to gasp.

"Can you tell me where the hospital is?" I asked her. "I'll take you."

"Yes," she gasped again.

Without much effort, I scooped her up and carried her to my van. Once I had her buckled into the passenger's seat, I ran around and got in. I already had the vents set for recirculate, so I put on the A/C, hoping it would revive her a bit. She did not look good. Green ropes of snot were starting to crawl down onto her upper lip from her nose, and her eyes were crusting over. Still, the A/C seemed to help her enough to let her give me directions to the hospital.

Π

I never did find out the name of the hospital, because we couldn't get anywhere near it. The place looked like a sold-out Rolling Stones concert. It was total gridlock—even ambulances were stuck in the throng trying to get to that hospital. "Shit," I said to myself. Then I looked over at Counter-Girl and realized she was either passed out or dead. I put my palm on her forehead and pushed her into an upright position. After a minute, she drew in a raspy breath and I knew my van hadn't yet become a hearse.

I managed to get out of that throng of vehicles, cross a median, and head back toward the station where I'd gotten gas and my allergic passenger. As I drove I noticed that Counter-Girl, in spite of her slimy malady, was actually quite a cutie-pie. (Most middle-aged men have a weakness for pretty young girls, and those who say they don't are either pedophiles, priests, congressmen, or just simple liars.)

If out of nothing more than a desire not to waste the potential of a cute young lady, I decided to do my best to save Counter-Girl. I drove back by the convenience store with grabbing a box of Benadryl on my mind. As I pulled in, I noticed there were no other cars there except my passenger's. Just as I was climbing out of my van, a kid came running out of the store with a bag of candy and a forty-ounce beer. As he flew past me, I could hear him wheezing.

"Beer'll just make that wheeze worse," I called after him.

He shot me a finger behind his back, and I went inside to get the Benadryl.

Π

About a mile or so down the road from Counter-Girl's gas station, was an old motel —what used to be referred to as a *Motor Court*. It was called The Pumpkin Coach Inn. The office was manned by a little old lady in a wheelchair with an oxygen bottle standing next to her. A clear-plastic mask was elasticed over her nose and mouth. "Got a room?" I asked.

"Got all of 'em," she said through her respirator. "Want one?"

As I was signing her register, I noticed she had a TV back there with her. "Got any idea what's going on at the hospital?" I asked, nodding my head toward her boob tube.

"Hay fever," she told me with a big smile on her face. "People droppin' like flies. It's all over the news. Don't bother me none," she added, patting her oxygen bottle. "I got the emphysema."

Π

Having been a child during the '60's, I decided to treat this pollen inundation as if it were radioactive fallout. After getting Counter-Girl out of my van and onto her feet, I retrieved my whisk-broom from under my seat and brushed as much of that green fallout off her, and myself, as possible. Then I put her onto one of the two beds in room six of The Pumpkin Coach Inn.

From the back of my van, I grabbed a roll of black, pro-grade duct tape. Then I took the sheets off the other bed and wet them down in the shower, taking care to leave the outside edges dry. After taping one of the sheets over the door, I checked the room's lone window. It was fixed, unopenable, so I used the other wet sheet to loosely drape the air conditioner/heater coming out of the wall under the window. Then I turned it on full bore and watched my designer-sheet pollen-catcher billow out.

"Take that, you commies," I said out loud, getting into the spirit of my nuclear fantasy.

Counter-Girl was wheezing heavily on the bed—her eyes a rheumy mess, and snot befouling her pretty face. After cleaning her up with a wet washcloth, I coaxed her to take two Benadryl and wash them down with my new Coke slushy. Caffeine, I knew, was also good for hay fever—like a little shot of adrenalin.

It was while pouring slushy down my patient that I noticed her clothes still had a fair tint of green to them. The room we were in seemed free of the offending substance, and the musty smell told me it was because it hadn't been used in a while. To keep the place fallout free, I stripped Counter-Girl down to her bra and panties, and threw her clothes into the bathtub. Then I ran the shower over them and watched little rivulets of green go down the drain.

Since I was going to have to repeat this procedure with my own clothes, I peeled back my door-sheet enough to get out and grab my suitcase from the van. I brought a wet towel with me to wipe it down with before I re-entered the room. By the time I had my clothes rinsed off and both our sets of garments wrung out and hanging over chairs and towel racks, Counter-Girl seemed to be breathing a tiny bit easier. The Benadryl, however, had put her soundly to sleep.

With nothing better to do, I propped myself up on the de-sheeted bed and clicked on the television. The news was grim, and seemed almost as frightening as my nuclear fantasy would have been were it to become reality. As I flipped from channel to channel, news service to news service, I gleaned the gist of it as best I could.

Apparently, pollen—mostly *tree* pollen, some were saying—had decided suddenly to mutate. One swollen-eyed, sneezing scientist on CNN explained that tree pollen is actually too large to cause much of an allergic reaction, but the mutation was making this too-large tree-pollen exude its own *micro*-pollen—as if it were a plant itself and not pollen at all. This so-called micro-pollen was so irritating to the human system it was causing toxic shock and other such nasty reactions in ninety-nine percent of the populations exposed to it. They were actually reporting *death tolls* on these news outlets, and though the numbers varied from channel to channel, the word catastrophic could certainly be used to describe even the most conservative of these estimates.

It wasn't long before I'd had enough of this horror story, so, out of curiosity, I changed over to the Weather Channel. Believe it or not, the swollen-faced announcer was standing in front of a satellite view of a pollen cloud drifting west out of Africa.

"Similar clouds," he was saying as he tried unsuccessfully to clear his throat, "are rising out of South America, Australia, and the Pacific Northwest."

"Fuck me," I said as I clicked off the tube. Then a startling realization washed over me that seemed well overdue. *I must be immune!* Oh, sure, I could *feel* it—it was a little irritating, but I was breathing just fine. Suddenly, Charlton Heston's face filled my mind's eye, and all I could think about was that movie, *Omega Man*. And for just an instant, a bizarre excitement ran through me like a static charge. What if I could pretty much have the world to myself? What if Counter-Girl's abandoned convenience store became the norm?

Trying to keep my sense of morality unskewed, I pushed those thoughts up against the back of my skull. But before I managed to line them up against the bone wall of my head, one of them called out, "You're gonna want a girl to keep you company if you're the last man on Earth!"

Π

I looked over at Counter-Girl, who had begun wheezing badly again. I'd pulled a sheet over her, but decided it couldn't hurt to uncover her and have a peek—just to see how her breathing looked and, you know, to check for rashes. As I slowly peeled back that cover, I saw her breathing was very labored, no rashes were apparent, and she definitely looked good enough to eat. Her skin was the color of French vanilla CoffeeMate, and her slight frame supported a lovely ass and what seemed, under their bra, to be a full grown, but not overly buxomous, pair of tits. It took me a good minute to insist to myself that her bra was *not* restricting her breathing. Something, however, was. Despite all my efforts, Counter-Girl was not getting any better. I was going to have to take drastic measures.

Π

I thought for a minute to put something on over the boxer shorts I was clad in, but decided against it. It would be much easier, when I came back in, to simply shower off than to have to rinse another set of clothes. Slipping out under the door-sheet, I made my way to the office of The Pumpkin Coach Inn. When the old lady saw me enter, she looked me over once, standing there in my boxers, and said, "Whatever you got in mind, I probably ain't got the breath for it."

Before I go on, I need to make something clear about moral priorities. Everyone knows that under certain extreme conditions—like war, or calamities of a more God-given nature—morality changes. And under conditions like these, even men who normally wouldn't steal gas from the blood-sucking oil companies, could be forced to commit what might usually be seen as heinous acts.

The woman in the wheelchair was old. She'd lived a life and was now feeble and diseased. My poor little, dying Counter-Girl had barely reached her prime. I hopped over the counter and plucked the breathing mask off the old lady. "What the fuck!" she screamed, as I threw her oxygen bottle over my shoulder. As I was leaving, I saw her going for the telephone, but she was already starting to choke. I propped open the door to the office and let the warm, green-laden breeze infiltrate her domain.

I could hear her finger poking nine, one and one on her phone. I smiled at the dismayed look on her face and said, "It's busy, isn't it?" I could hear her diseased lungs pretty much coming apart as I headed back to my fallout shelter.

Π

Counter-Girl's name turned out to be Shelly. The old lady's oxygen did wonders for her, and once she found out what was going on in the world, she was very appreciative of my ministrations. She realizes I have to keep her in that room, but I bring her all sorts of toys and goodies to keep her occupied. And when I come back from my scavenging trips, she likes to keep *me* occupied.

Just the other day, her pee turned a little pregnancy-test strip blue, which means I'm going to be a daddy. I'm hoping my child inherits my immunity to tree-pollen pollen. If not, he or she will have to keep Mommy company inside The Pumpkin, which is getting larger as I knock out the walls between rooms.

There's no TV or radio anymore, and I've had to wire generators up to the motel. Every once in a while I see another human being on my foraging trips, all of whom have seemed to me to be quite happy and contented. Whether it was the trees or God or just good genes, something liked us enough to bless us and give us the world.

I like to think it was the trees who, in their silent wisdom, rid their planet of all but a manageable few of the hideous infestation known as mankind. Or, who knows, maybe it *was* God—drowning humanity once again, only this time in a sea of plant semen. I guess you could call that a fucking apocalypse. Fallout of a divine nature.

The End

Dharma And Bert

by
Marshall Payne

When Dharma returned to her elemental palace of reconstituted fire and ice, she instantly felt the memories of the old estate. She'd been voidriding for the past countless aeons and to wear the flesh again was a strange admixture of sweet unadulterated oxygen and painful birth-slap on her divine derrière. Oblivion was not at all what her sisters had promised her it would be. Even wrapped in a cocoon of nullification she had still felt something—*dammit!* —when what she had bargained for was conscious nonexistence. Was that too much to ask?

Having been gone from the palace for so long, she was easily susceptible to the lingering sensations of soirées long passed. Of the time Ruby Blue had challenged her three-score-plus-two husbands in a dual to the death with one another. (Dharma never could remember which hapless sod had been the victor.) Or when she had slept with Daphne on a lark just to prove the point that men were a necessary evil. Or when Klea had hanged herself in the east wing when she was in one of her rare let's-try-falling-in-love moods. Dharma had been the one to cut her down. After her resurrection Klea admitted that it had been a pointless experiment and that she'd never try it again. Oh the memories! In this very mansion Dharma had lost and regained her virginity so many times she'd lost count. So why had she returned? Daphne, who considered herself something of a philosopher of jocularity, once said, "Immortality wouldn't be so bad if it didn't go on forever." Truer words were never spoken.

Dharma was one of the chosen, one of the sacrosanct Goddesses of Love. For aeons she'd stood by her pantheon through good times and bad, her sisterhood, Klea, Daphne, Ruby Blue, and herself. Together they toyed with men's hearts, minds, pocketbooks, and sexual proclivities. Between the four of them they were *the* Mistresses of all they surveyed, and with a multiplicity of universes out there to choose from, that covered an extensive turf.

Klea was the youngest of the group, feisty, petite, strawberry blonde. What she lacked in years, she more than made up for in impropriety. She had always referred to their elite coterie as The Pantheon of Bitches, a locution that irritated Ruby Blue. But of course Klea had often proclaimed herself as the Empress of the Vulgarian Empire, promising that when she had the time (and patience) she would settle her own system of suns and terraform a host of worlds to explore and exploit her own debaseness. "A whole race of Vulgarians," she'd said. "Can you imagine it?" But no one took her seriously. Even with her deadly encounter with love, she couldn't manage to tie her own noose.

And then there was Daphne, the pragmatic one with an intellectual bent. She believed sex and love were the only two building blocks of all the universes, and that once those two components were properly "mastered" (Oh! how she hated the masculinity of that word, but "mistressed" didn't work at all in that context), creation would spawn creation like a virus in a tepid pond. But men were definitely not quintessential to the equation, she maintained. And after allowing herself to be hurt by one of them needlessly, she'd converted to Lesbianism and pronounced it the acme of all religions. "All men are scum!" she proclaimed, and soon had invented the term "scumette," which she'd called Dharma one night when the cunnilingus wasn't up to her high standard. But in later years she became of the mindset that spiritual transcendence could only be achieved through total deconstructionism. So, she'd turned to sloth. The last Dharma heard of her she was caught between dimensions, needle and spoon on one side, counsel to inertia on the other.

And finally there was Ruby Blue, most seductive of immortal, immoral sirens. She was convinced she was the True Mother of the Daughters of Joy, a high-baud strumpet who had reinvented the world's oldest profession. Without so much as a rune or magic potion, she had turned herself from a B-girl in Philly to a virtuoso of the concubinal arts. Yes, she understood the whys and wherefores of these things, or so she claimed. Men had been created by women to wage wars, conquer star systems, or, if they were of limited scope like husband #37, to die of a heart attack in a brightly tiled men's room on Wall Street, nitroglycerin tablet in hand. The rumor mill had it that she had purposely dethroned herself and was working 42nd Street these days, grinding out a marginal existence at twenty dollars a trick. Oh, how the mighty had fallen.

All of the above reasons were why Dharma had ultimately left the sisterhood. Together they comprised a tragedy greater than the sum of its parts. They had become bizarre, obtuse, decadent--truly weird sisters. Toward the end they'd each been unable to cope with even the simplest realities. It was as if their motto were: *If it's obviously broken, then why not fix something else?*

Anyway, as Dharma stood in her empty palace feeling the vibrations of soirées long past, she now knew why she had left the sisterhood and became a voidrider. Though imperfect, oblivion had helped shield her not only from the disappointments of coitus, but from love, hate, fear, pain, envy . . . It gave her an existence devoid of promise and passion. But here now in her palace of fire and ice, she found the ice could still freeze her heart, and the fire still burn her fingertips. Now all her past glories were assaulting her at once; but the flame couldn't melt the ice and the ice couldn't extinguish the flame. And the craving was once again upon her!

So she inhaled deeply, sniffing out her demons. There was a man in the palace! she realized with horror. How long had he been here? Had he simply moved in and made himself at home in her absence?

She ran from bedroom to bedroom, looking for socks and underwear scattered on the floor. Nothing. She ran to the main bathroom. The toilet seat was still down, but no telltale droplets of pee were present. Strange. She could definitely smell the man-creature. His pheromones wafting through the air. His after-shave. His maleness hanging like a thick masculine fog. But then she had to consider the possibility that it was all in her imagination. Had her own insatiable desires imprinted these sensations on the fabric of reality? Had her aeons of suppressed longing given birth to these traceries, insubstantial proofs of her wanton passions?

It didn't matter now, however. The jones was upon her. She had to have a man. Maybe she could contact Klea, Daphne, or Ruby Blue for assistance. But Klea was probably off hanging from another noose somewhere and there was no time to resurrect her. And Daphne was most likely following her own deconstructionist muse: short on men, long on inertia. That left Ruby Blue on 42nd Street. A possibility, but was she willing to stoop that low? No, she decided.

The passion filled her completely now. There was no turning back. There must be a man around here somewhere, she thought. There had been so many over the years it was hard to imagine that she couldn't scare one up somehow. And then she remembered. Didn't she have one in the dungeon?

She bounded down the stairs three steps at a time, summoning on the lights when reaching the bottom. The room was a huge damp cavern with remnants of yesterday's parties (empty bottles of booze, party favors, spent prophylactics used only as a novelty) all over the place. Where? she thought. She was sure she'd left one down there someplace.

The closet!

She opened the door and found him there, naked, slumped on the floor. Barry? Bob? Ben? Something like that. It had been so long. She had ordered him from a catalogue back when the sisterhood had been sampling a cheesy sci-fi motif during a period of extreme ennui. (Ray guns, phallic-shaped rocket ships, deep-space monsters, jut-jawed heroes, and one mechanical man.) Anything to break the monotony. The man had only been purchased as a joke, but now she didn't care.

As she pulled his grease-spotted body from the closet she heard the kerosene sloshing around inside of him. Even for a goddess with unlimited power, he was heavy, but at least he was still in one piece. She laid him on the concrete floor and turned him on his side. On the nape of his neck was a small metal plate that said BERT. Well, she'd been close.

"Okay, Bert," she said aloud, though she felt rather foolish talking to him until she got him running, "let's see if we can get you started."

She pulled back a flap of skin above his left buttock and found the pull cord. She hoped he had enough oil. After turning up the fuel valve, she pulled the cord. *Rup rup rup rup rup* as the engine tried to catch. She tried it again, but nothing. She knew there was fuel in him; she'd heard the kerosene sloshing and she could smell the harsh fumes. And then she realized that she hadn't turned on the choke. After doing so she tried it again. More *rup rups* but he still didn't turn over. She was getting angry. Horny and angry.

"What's your fucking problem, Bert!" she screamed at the man-contraption. "I command you to ignite!"

She pulled the cord again, this time pulling as hard as she could and he finally sputtered to life. Dark smoke chuffed out his mouth and anus as the engine caught. She turned off the choke and adjusted the throttle. Bert sat up and opened his eyes. "Stand up, Bert," she commanded.

He shambled to his feet with a series of clumsy jerks, trying to maintain his balance. But when she commanded him to have an erection, he wasn't able to rise to the occasion. He just looked at her with sad eyes, his flaccid muscles quivering to the rumble of his engine. He opened his mouth and tried to speak, but she couldn't hear his voice. "What did you say?" she asked.

His lips moved again. "I-I love you," he stuttered.

Suddenly Dharma was filled with rage. "You can't love me!" she screamed. She reached out and knocked him to the ground with both hands and began kicking him furiously. "I should rape and murder you, you bastard! You can't love me! There's no way you can love, got it? You're just a machine!"

When she finally stopped kicking him, she noticed that a drop of machine oil had teared from his eye. He was panting heavily, pretending that he was breathing, when in actuality he was—he needed oxygen to function as did she. He rolled over on his back and looked up at her.

"I could love you if you would teach me how," Bert said, his voice imploring.

She leaned over him. "Don't you understand, I can't teach you what I don't know myself?" But he didn't say anything. He just lay there, panting, chuffing out black soot. Obviously Bert was in need of repair—a tune-up at the very least. She wondered why she had allowed herself to get so upset over this mechanical man. She'd only bought him as a party gag in the first place.

By now her rage had passed, and so had her libidinal craving. Not knowing what else to do, she went to find a tool box. Although she had never been very mechanically inclined, she knew she had one around there somewhere. She had a lot of work ahead of her.

The End

Hundred Year Old Murders

by
Garrett Cook

I.

It had been awhile since Frankie the Priest lost his job. His collar was tainted by a drop of phantom semen from the liaison with the governor's son. Half mad, he wandered the streets, staring through wolfish eyes at the pretty young boys. He usually didn't pay the women much attention —sinful things, all dark caverns, monthly blood and secrets. Yet, the strange, ripe blonde caught his eye; she seemed as out of place as he was; as desperate, feral and confused. For one thing, she wore no clothes at all as she made her propositions. A shilling for her softness, a shilling for a night, but this was Pittsburgh and nobody knew the exchange rates, or else they could find their own whores.

She dodged the cops like a pro, mugger or alley cat, always knowing the darkest, safest place to disappear to, as though she could know no other home, as though birthed by bubbling asphalt. He bought her a Whopper and a cup of coffee and having gained her trust, brought her to the man for whom he sometimes did work. From serving god, he'd gone down several rungs.

Tommy Shovels was called that because of all the men he buried. He wasn't a killer, but he had to do what he had to. And this time he gave up a twelve year old boy, a gift to the priest for scouting her out. Even a shit like Frankie the Priest deserved something for his time.

II.

She was a poetess in the snuff film. She made all the other girls look like amateurs, though of course there can only be amateurs working in snuff. Each twitch beneath the cattle prod was perfection, the hint of perverse joy at every slap of her face was delicious. Her gaze of anguish brought July-wind warmth and goosebumps in places Tommy barely knew existed. It was a shame the gunshot would have to cut everything short, but when it came, the gunshot was gorgeous as well.

There was neither fear or surprise, just a "goodnight daddy" look that reminded him of his cheerleader daughter. He hated that he could only do one tape.

III.

Two days later, she was pristine. There was not a drop of blood or grave dirt when the priest found her on the same street. If he wasn't half mad, he wouldn't have thought it was her, but being as far gone as he was, he couldn't admit another possibility. She had the same blonde hair, same tricks for a shilling, same accent, same curves, same programmed bestial streetwise whenever a cop was in sight. He had known of resurrection happening once, a favor from God, the return of His Son, and Frankie the priest felt that God had forgiven his sins, rewarded his devotion and granted him a means to get what he needed. He was thankful to God as he gave her another Whopper and cup of coffee. She acted as if she knew him, which was odd, but through God, all things were possible. He took the boy for three days this time, charging for the miracle he'd received.

The cast of the film took her brutally, one at a time, and though she begged them to stop, she still took them like an expert. When the first round was done, they took her two at a time for half an hour before she began to grow weak. She ended the snuff film looking beatific, though she was put down like a tired greyhound when they'd had her fill. She smiled with her throat slit and pressed her ample breasts together seductively as she said her goodbye to the earth.

IV.

Like the cat from the old song, she came back the very next day, picked up by Tommy Shovels so he wouldn't have to reward the priest. As Tommy Shovels drove her to the warehouse where he filmed, his mind was swimming with ideas and possibilities. He thought of the things he'd seen in old horror movies and the things he dreamt of doing to his ex-wife for running off and leaving him alone with his daughter. Where once there was a killer and a pornographer, there was something of an artist. And the girl performed admirably as this artist emerged; she thrilled with fear and ecstasy as she was exsanguinated by syringes. The anguish on her face was a Munch lithograph as she was burned alive. Tommy Shovels couldn't be held back any longer. He knew that the men who bought snuff films did not deserve bliss like this, so decided it was time to go mainstream.

The trial raged on for a great long time over whether freedom of speech was even a factor, but since she was neither alive nor dead, the sublime Miss Mary Jane Kelly was a valid target for slaughter and molestation, an acceptable scapegoat for the rage and sexual frustrations of a confused America. So, Tommy Shovels rose to the top.

V.

In his London home, Jack the Ripper beamed as he read in Variety of the slaughtered whore and her ascent to stardom. He paced the floors of his house all hours of the night, remembering her scent, her beauty and how she looked as bits of meat laid out upon a nightstand. He got on his coat and deerstalker, flying to Los Angeles in search of the only angel he wanted.

VI.

When Tommy Shovels came home with his Oscar and his actress slash fiancée, he was met by two surprises: his disemboweled teenage daughter lain out on the coffee table in the living room and an English gentleman covered in blood and vaginal secretions standing over her triumphantly. The Englishman cleared his throat and delivered a little speech.

"I will not kill you, boss. See, I'm no queer, but Saucy Jack wants back what he holds dear."

Tommy Shovels ran screaming from the mansion and was never heard from again by anyone.

"Forgive me?" Jack asked, handing Mary a bunch of grapes.

Though uncertain what living with Tommy would do for her career, Mary still wrapped her arms around her dripping id of a destiny.

"We belong together, Jack."

Turned out, Mary did not need to fear for her career. Their unfortunate separation had given Jack time to ponder a century of brilliant cruelties. A new Golden Age of cinema was born.

The End

The Groin Scratcher

by
Rhys Hughes

He was English and he lived in a quaint old village and his name was Peter the Tenant and nobody ever suggested he was a sexual pervert. His erotic tastes were fairly normal: he was faithful to his girlfriend and fucked her twice a day and spurted his cream in her quim almost exclusively. On special occasions, such as his cock's birthday, he used her mouth and sprayed the back of her throat. Very rarely he wanked himself off between her tits but never did he penetrate her bumhole. In other words he was an unremarkable example of mister average and only the fact his cock was a different age to the rest of him betrayed his unique status among his fellow men.

He attended some of my creative writing classes and produced a few mediocre texts and that's high praise indeed coming from me, Mr Gum, the most vindictive and resentful tutor on the nightschool run, not that I play that game these days. No, I retired from teaching and went into business with Fellatio Nelson, a much more profitable affair, and I've never looked back, apart from those few occasions when implausible necessity compelled me to bend over without trousers. Yes, I like to see what's coming in such situations. My business partner's style is quite different: he just likes to get his head down and not make eye contact with any mode of expression.

Did you appreciate that seemingly clever sentence? It's an example of my virtuosity in the art of arranging words in a straight line, a particular talent of mine, one you probably don't possess, and if you care to argue with that I'll set Fellatio Nelson on you. Then you'll be sorry and very sore. But there's no need for all this resentment and hostility, dear reader, so let's return to the issue of Peter the Tenant. He was born with a cock like any other man but dated its birth from his first erection, acquired while sliding down a banister at increasing velocity towards an ornamental knob at the terminus of the stairway. That's why man and dangly were different ages. The knob snapped off.

My own views on ornamental knobs are not widely known but I plan to write a short treatise on the subject in due course. One day the works of Mr Gum will dominate all other kinds of literature: just you wait! Anyway the penile dating system of Peter the Tenant had its own peculiar advantages and dis-advantages, the listing of which might prove profitable but probably won't. His first erection occurred during his tenth summer. By the time Peter was twenty-five years old his cock was still underage for legal intercourse and any girl who introduced it into her quim was risking arrest. Having said that, how does one put handcuffs on a pussy? There must be a knack to it.

Luckily for all concerned, our unsynchronised hero has now passed his fortieth birthday and his girlfriend is only thirty, so cock and cunt are peers. Notice the subtle shift from past to present tense? You're such a genius, Mr Gum, yes I am. I might even shift the text into the future tense. Don't believe me? *You will* . . . Anyway, the girlfriend of our Peter was a sweet and willing conjuror's assistant by the name of Claribell Teddyface. We are all conjurors' assistants in this great illusion called life, but that's just metaphysical claptrap. Claribell was the real thing. She had assisted the Fructuous Grapevine on the cabaret circuit and picked up a few tricks from her master in the process.

If you've never heard of the Fructuous Grapevine, which is highly likely since I just invented him, don't bother seeking him out. His act wasn't worth the admission price, to say nothing of the fact that he died recently. Cows crushed him while he was walking between rural outposts of the aforementioned cabaret circuit. A cretinous farmer was listening to the radio and mistook the words of a Marvin Gaye song for a divine command. Without pausing to consider the awfulness of the pun and the damage it might do to *my* reputation when I related it, he calmly proceeded to 'herd it on the grapevine'. Bones splintered, blood spurted, organs were squashed as flat as solid puddles of leaked tractor oil.

Without her master to pay her, and occasionally use her as a vessel for his seed, Claribell wandered in search of fresh opportunities. Somehow she met Peter the Tenant: I can't be bothered to invent the details of that encounter, so do it yourself if you think it necessary. Every morning and evening he came in her quim. I've already mentioned that, but I like the word 'quim' and have no scruples about repeating myself in order to write it again. If my name wasn't Mr Gum I would like to be called Sir Quim or something along those juicy lines. But let's not get deliciously distracted. Peter the Tenant was also a conjuror, an amateur but quite skilled, and so they were well matched in bed and elsewhere.

The first time they slept together turned out to be a magical occasion. He peeled off her clothes until she was left only in her panties but she restrained him from going further with the words "It's my time of the month" to which Peter responded "I don't really care". So the final item of clothing was removed, Claribell lay back with spread legs and reached down to pull the string that would remove her tampon. Out it came with a crimson slurp. Peter was about to plunge into the recently vacated space but Claribell rummaged inside and produced a second tampon, then a third and fourth. "Presto!" she cried each time. The tampons kept coming, like butchered bunnies out of a rubbery top hat. Soon there were a hundred of them.

Peter the Tenant waited impatiently for the trick to finish. When the last tampon was removed he clapped politely and threw himself on top of her. Cock slid into pussy like a mutilated hand into a deformed glove. Have you ever done that, dear reader? Mr Gum has: he's not a stinking virgin! That's me, by the way. Anyway, Peter panted these words into Claribell's ear: "Now I'm going to show you a trick of my own." And so he did. He began thrusting back and forth in the standard human manner, but on each thrust he slid his body up along hers. He was clearly using his cock to saw her in half along her longitudinal axis. What a sore puss saw pussy! She gasped while he rasped. Imperfect symmetry.

Eventually he reached the top of her head and the bisection was completed. He stood up, bone dust making him sneeze, and eased the two halves of her body apart. Then he walked around the bed, bowing to an invisible audience, before replacing the left and right sides. A few shakes of a bedsheet and some mumbled magic words and Claribell Teddyface was a whole woman again, though the incision never healed completely and still leaked pus whenever he brought her to orgasm. That was their inaugural fuck. And if you believe that, you really are a gullible gimp. No, of course it didn't happen that way. How could it? No man's cock is serrated, not even Marvin Gaye's, to say nothing of the fact that Claribell's pussy never opened without the correct security code.

That's right. Plunging straight into *her* quim is out of the question. A four digit personal identification number has to be inputted before her labial lips juice up and part. Otherwise she remains clammed up tighter than a rusty singularity at the centre of an iron black hole. I can throw in some physics if I please: I'm Mr Gum! Now then. Claribell whispered the relevant code to Peter the Tenant and he told it to me and I don't mind passing it to you right now. It went like this: clockwise tongue lick on the left nipple, ditto on the right, middle finger in the belly button, knuckle rap on the pubic bone. Do that and you're in. Peter did it often, always with a backward glance to make sure nobody was spying on the sequence.

One evening the procedure felt different from normal, slightly strange, the nipples a little rougher, the belly button less deep, the pubic bone more metallic. But he didn't take much notice because her quim opened for him without fuss. In he went, humped the required number of times, ejaculated. Then he rolled over and fell asleep. All night he was plagued by involuntary orgasms of horrendous intensity and duration. He woke in a sweat, inputted the security code, fucked Claribell again, but this morning his sperm was less creamy and deployed into her pussy with less power. The day began properly. The involuntary orgasms continued, dwindling in force, disappearing for good in the late afternoon. Peter the Tenant limped back home. A curious emptiness clanged wetly inside his soul like a bell with a tampon clapper.

The evening passed unremarkably with his girlfriend. Then it was bedtime. He threw her down on the sheets, applied the security code, slid in and pumped. But nothing came. Try as he might, no sperm emerged. Finally he had to pull out and make his apologies. Claribell was tolerant but when the same thing happened in the morning she couldn't hide her annoyance. "I'm going through a dry patch," Peter gasped, "so give me some time to get over it." Yes, Claribell was happy to do that. But the sperm never returned. Peter modified his diet to increase his potency: he ate ginseng salads with horny goat weed garnish and Spanish Fly dressing. But his tanks never refilled. Finally he rang the local branch of his sperm bank to check his account.

"You are clean out of come," came the reply.

"But I had enough spunk in there to last a lifetime! How has my account been drained? I limit myself to two fucks a day," protested Peter.

"Not according to the data on the screen in front of me," the anonymous voice insisted. "It seems you spent all your savings in just twelve hours. Fifty gallons went on a bukkake competition, another twenty on spit-roasting, ten on glory holes, another ten on prostate milking and the final ten on erotic asphyxiation. That makes one hundred gallons in total, the upper limit of your lifetime allowance. Sir, you have been fucked."

"But how could this happen? None of those orgasms were mine!"

"Clearly you are the victim of fraudsters. Sometimes they fit false erogenous zones over a man's girlfriend that look just like the real thing. That's how they get access to personal identification codes. You need to be alert for anything unusual when operating a lady's nipples and clitoris. This is a common problem for sperm banks. Don't panic. You might not have lost all your spunk forever. Maybe we can reimburse you."

Hope glittered in Peter's eyes. "Really? How?"

"We need to take some personal details, sir. Firstly, may I have your date of birth?"

"Certainly. 24th November 1954."

"Hmm ... ah! Well yes ... but ... I'm sorry, that's not the date I have listed under your cock's signature. There's quite a discrepancy ... "

"Wait! It's easily explained. My cock's birthday is different from my own. Let's see. 2nd July 1964. Just before teatime. On the banister. Is that right? Please don't hang up!"

A flicker of movement violated the edges of Peter's vision. He turned to confront Claribell who had packed a suitcase and was preparing to leave. "This pussy needs milk!" she sneered before storming out the door. All was lost. Peter hesitated between girlfriend and telephone. Then he raised the mouthpiece and said, "I want to close my account. I don't need it anymore." But the tone was already dead.

To prove I'm a man of integrity and courage as well as enormous talent, I ought to confess that Peter the Tenant doesn't really exist, or rather he *does* exist but isn't who he claims to be. His real name is Hymen Simon and he's a dwarf or animated puppet made from a burst maidenhead. He played a vile trick on me once and this is my revenge: telling the world about the time his balls went dry forever.

In fact I was the one responsible for draining them. With plenty of help from Fellatio Nelson, of course. I told you we went into business together but I never specified our work was *legal*, did I? Not at all! In fact we are fraudsters, the pair of us, and we specialise in fitting false erogenous zones on female bodies. Getting access to those bodies is the difficult part. I knock on doors like a regular salesman and offer the services of the finest Creative Writing tutor in history. While the housewives are distracted by my banter, Fellatio Nelson skilfully attaches the fake zones. He's good at that, stealthy as a snake:

probably because he once had a serpentine cock. I broke that in another story. Things other than banister knobs do snap off, you know.

I've lost count of the number of personal security codes we've managed to obtain in this devious manner, spending the seed of other men on our own sexual experiences. An endless supply of sperm is ours for the spurting. But I regard the theft of Peter the Tenant's entire stock of jism as my most malicious, and therefore greatest triumph. Left without a girlfriend he would have turned to masturbation for solace. But without cream to spill, what is the point of wanking? His solitary erotic pleasure now consists of obsessively scratching his groin with uncut fingernails.

This possibly puerile incident happened in the charmingly sordid village of Precome-on-Bum.

The End

Faux Pas, Doc

by
Janett L. Grady

I'm at the port in Paris, on my way to the port in Boston. My insides are all screwed up and I'm on my way to see if I can get things fixed. If I can't get things fixed, the conservative types in World Congress will order me taken apart and I'll be fed to the hogs, piece by piece. I'm three hours early for the transfer and I've already been scanned and labeled. I'm killing time, wandering back and forth, when I suddenly spot her, or think it's her. She's in one of those ancient hoverchairs. I wave, catch her eye and she waves back, hovers toward me, a quizzical, surprised look on her face.

"Well, well," she says with a smile. "What a surprise."

I smile in return. "Doc," I say, "it is you. My God, you haven't changed at all." It's almost true. She's in the chair, a few pounds heavier, a little older-looking but the same Doc Tan who turned me on back in 3010. "How have you been?" I ask. "It's been what, twenty years?"

"At least that long," she says. She hovers back a little and looks me up and down, her blue eyes crinkling at the corners. She's gorgeous. Even after all these years, I still want to give her a great big kiss. "Damn, T-3," she says, "you're looking fine." She sighs and then frowns prettily. "I never thought you'd last this long," she says. "Is it all still working?"

"Still working," I tell her, and hesitate, unsure about telling her what's wrong. "I'm at the Capitol," I tell her. "I've been there for nine years."

"Men, women, or what?" she asks. "You're wired for both, or at least I tried." She laughs. "But with all the women in World Congress these days, I wouldn't be all that surprised if you've been rewired to prefer women."

"You're right," I tell her. "I still do men, but I've been tweaked to prefer women."

"I figured they might do that," she says. "But, hey, no big deal, right?"

"It is a big deal," I shoot back. "When I do men, it hurts like hell. There's something wrong. I'm on my way to Mass Tech to see if I can get it fixed."

She doesn't seem interested. She

shrugs, looks at her watch. "I've got a few minutes," she says. "You want some wine?" She doesn't wait for an answer. She spins around, waves for me to follow, and leads the way into The French Space. She leaves me at a table, goes for the wine and then joins me. She sips from her glass, settles back in her chair. "You do look a little different," she says, "but hell, don't we all? Me, I'm stuck in this chair." Her eyes seem fixed on my blouse. "So what's wrong?" she asks. "You look healthy enough."

"I'm not," I tell her. "The penis-pocket is closing shut, not to mention being backed up. I'm not passing the way I should be."

"It's been a long time," she says. "You've been screwing your brains out, and you're scratched and swollen. It's the inside sensors. They wear out." She takes my hand, squeezes hard, then lets go. "Tell you what," she says. "I'm in the lab at Notre Dame. If they don't fix it in Boston, come back and let me know. I'll take a look." She grins a mischievous grin. "If worse comes to worse, " she says, "I'll take it all apart and start over. Then you can stay with me, service yours truly for awhile."

I'm sipping wine, biting my lip, trying to keep from looking at her. I can't stop thinking about her being in the chair and I don't want her to see any trace of fear on my face.

"So what's with the chair?" I ask. "If you don't mind me asking, I'd like to know what happened."

"Nothing much," she says. "A transport to Moscow didn't quite take and I lost the use of my legs. It's no big deal, though, I've still got feeling down there. You can kiss it and lap it and it'll drive me wild."

"I'd like that, Doc, but . . . "

"No buts," she says. "I'll clear it with Congress, let 'em know you're going to be with me." She glances at her watch, says she's got to run. "I'll be looking for you, T-3." She smiles that cute little smile of hers, waves and keeps waving as she hovers away. I assume she's hurrying to catch a transfer. "Doc, wait," I shout, but she's already gone.

My own transport doesn't happen for another hour, so I just sit there drinking wine. I'm thinking about how Doc is in a hoverchair, and figure if she can't fix herself, how in the hell is she going to fix me? True, she's the one who turned me on, but that was twenty years ago. It's not that I don't want to be at her beck and call, because in a way I always have. But Doc Tan has always been well connected with the anti-science, anti-sex types in Congress. Besides, if Doc is at Notre Dame, a man's world, it's my guess she'll simply take me apart, have me fed to the hogs, piece by piece, and start over. I'm not going to let her do it, no matter what. While I'm no longer a perfect toy for men, I'm still pretty good when it comes to women. I just need fixing, that's all.

Sorry, Doc, but I just don't trust you. For one thing, the inside of what you first designed and put together is now all screwed up. For another, I'm Tan Number 2, not Tan Number 3. T-2, not T-3.

The End

Highway Girl

by Robert Lamb

She was a dark-haired thing—small and pale, weak against his grip. He held her down by the wrists, gripping them both in one solid fist. With the other hand, he ripped her blouse open and liberated her soft tits from the black straps of her bra—soft dabbles of flesh against her ribcage. He squeezed them, prodded them, teased the thick nipples with sweaty pinches. God, he wanted to bite them. She screamed at him, kicked and squirmed as drops of his sweat dribbled down his hair and onto her face. His cock throbbed against his leg. He hiked up her skirt and tore at the white panties. Her legs thrashed horribly, but he finally slinked the soft cotton down her pale, bruised thighs.

He stared down greedily at her pubis, at the small dark triangle between her legs—so dark it didn't even seem like hair—like a bad airbrush job out of a stroke mag. He licked his fingers, reached down with his free hand to feel for that hidden soft ripple of flesh.

But all he touched was smooth glass.

There was a white flash of light.

"Bitch!"

Then darkness. He couldn't see! He screamed and released his grip, tumbled back on his ass against the brick wall. He pawed blindly at his eyes, at the bright splotches that pulsated across the black.

"Cunt! Fucking cunt!"

He felt around for her, palms scraping over rough, damp pavement. His foot kicked a crumpled beer can, sent it rattling down the alley.

The darkness finally began to clear and he looked up to see the blurred image of the girl standing over him—her skirt ripped, tits still poking through the crisscross of ruined blouse and bra.

"Now look, he said . . . " he said.

She replied—something completely incoherent. He hadn't remembered her voice being quite that annoying in the bar. Beer goggles, maybe. But now it was all screeching and grinding, all dental drills and fax machines.

She leaned over him and he felt a needle jab into his arm. Before he could realize what was happening, her small hand reached under his shirt, caressed his fat paunch. The skin began to tingle as she slathered it in some kind of jelly.

"What the fuck are—"

More mindless buzzing, the voice of gossiping circular saws and nagging tattoo needles. It must have been a lullaby, because he slept.

Nine months later, he gave birth to a healthy, 150-pound girl. Just like her mother, she was cold and distant. She had the same voice. The same incomprehensible nature.

And she was also out the door before he could try to understand her. At least her mom had given him a chance to say goodbye. He'd been high as a kite from the shit she'd pumped into his arm, and she probably hadn't heard him over the whirl and buzz of her own handiwork. But he'd thanked her, all the same, for the stitches and the dope.

In the chaos of the delivery room, he watched his daughter through the frame of his own hairy, stirrup-locked legs.

Her long black hair whipped behind her as she ran, her pale blood-speckled legs carrying her down the sterile-white hallway. She lashed out with one thin arm, instantly decapitating a security guard with fingers that twitched like a bundle of surgical tools. The head rolled into another room. Blood splashed the wall, sprayed onto the ceiling tiles and fluorescent bulbs as the body danced and fell.

The hallway was red.

Screams everywhere.

He shed a tear for her.

Wished her well.

Succumbed to blood loss.

'All Worldly Defences' by Dave Migman

'Behind the Mask' by Dave Migman

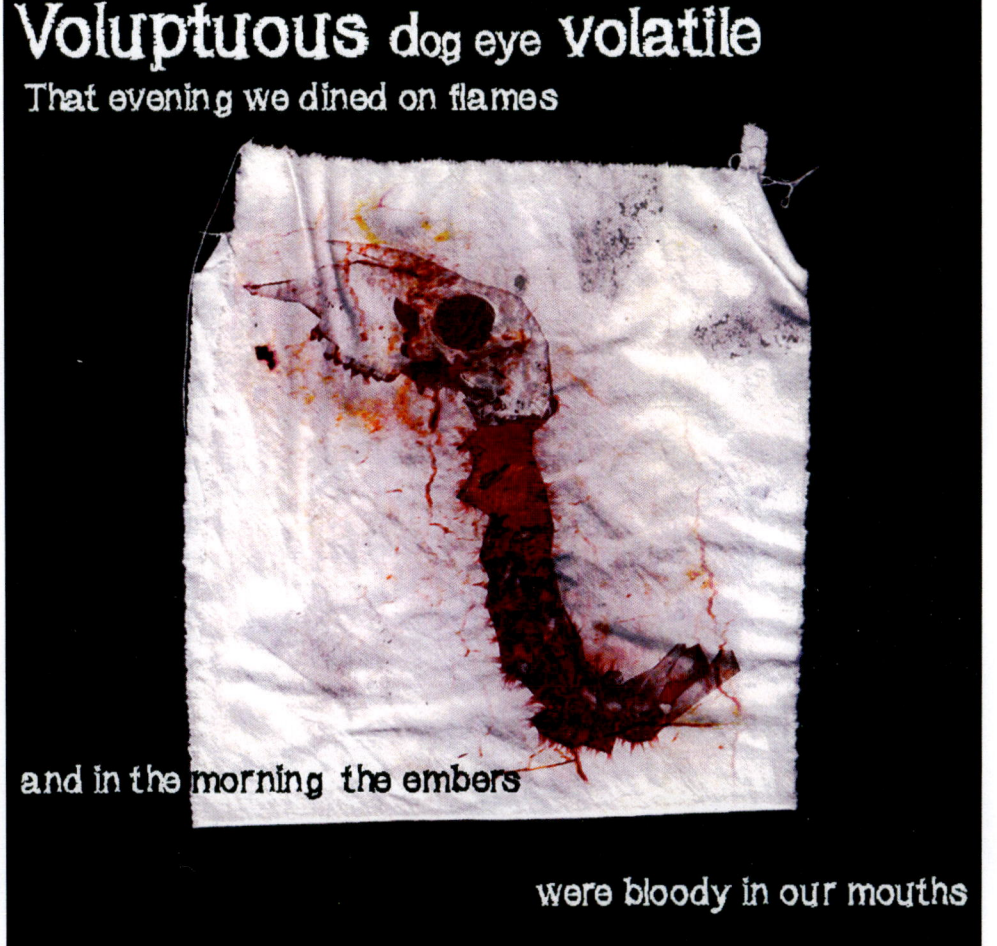

'Dog Eye Volatile' by Dave Migman

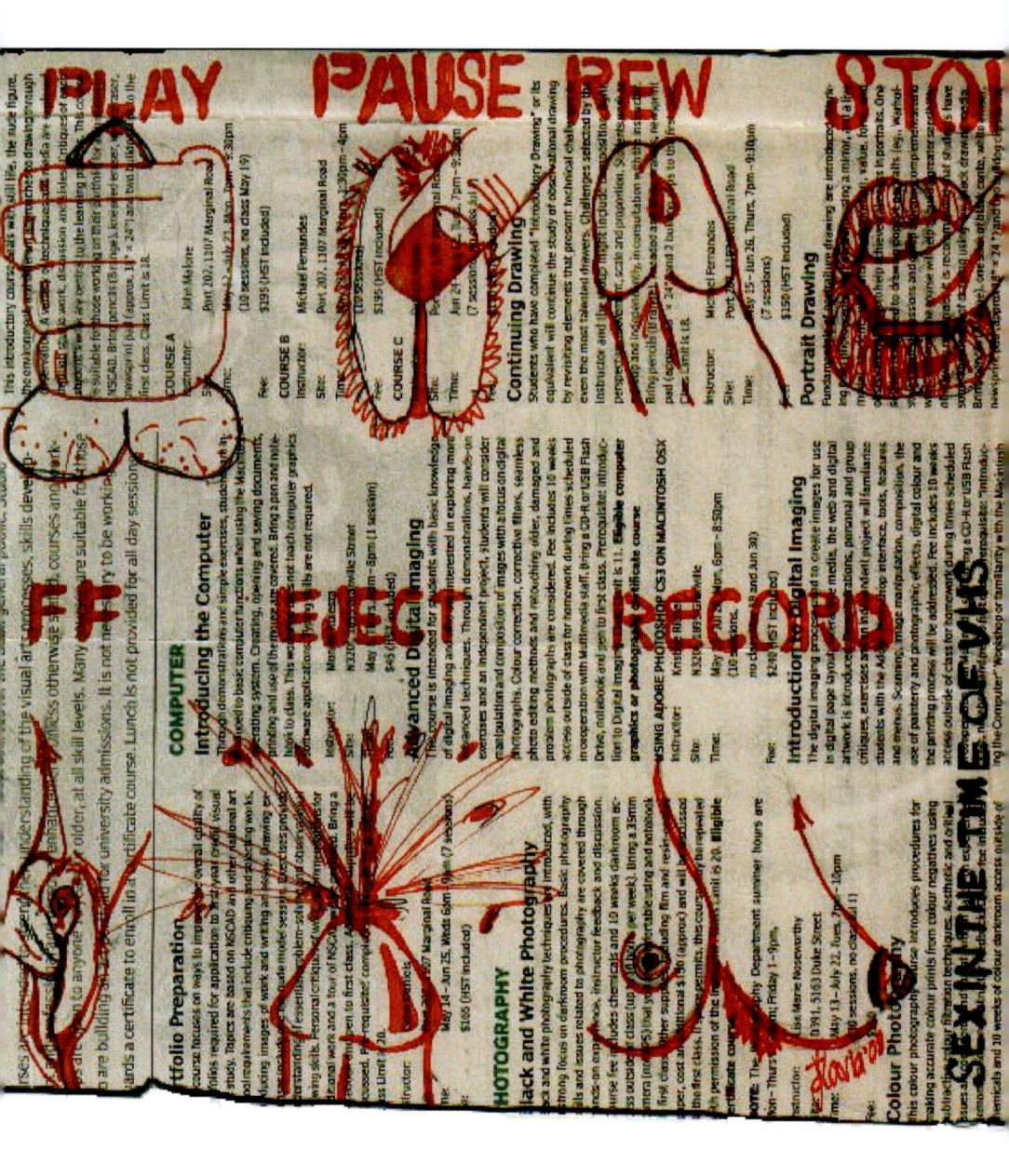

'Sex in the Time of VHS' by Flavia Testa-Lytle

'Time' by Dave Migman

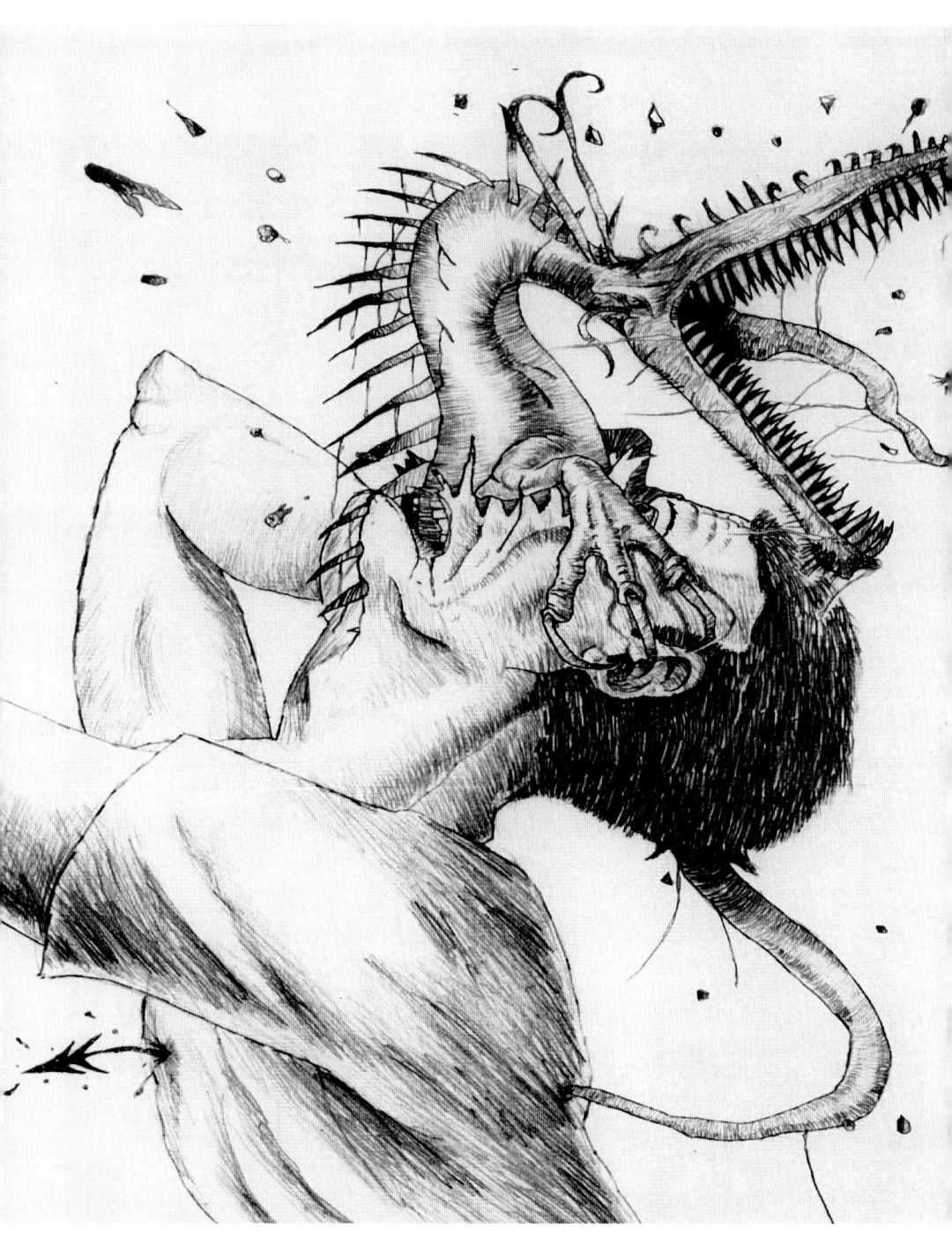

'Hate Song' by Dave M

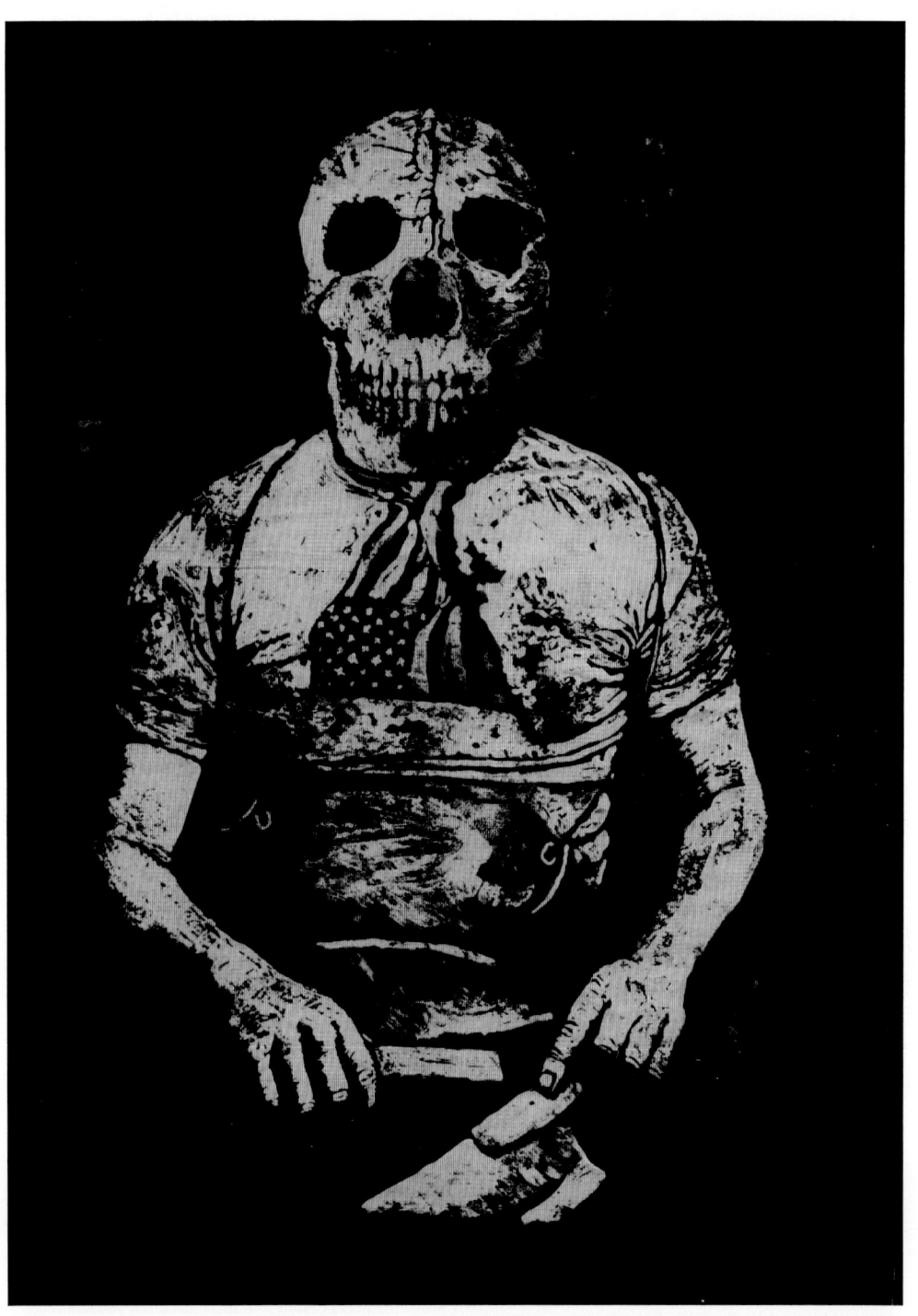

'World Bank Policy' by Dave Migman

The Last Taboo

by
Micci Oaten

I have just been interviewed by LOTL Magazine who have inspired me by their questions to write this piece. They interviewed myself and my girlfriend as we are part of an ITV/Virgin 1 show called "...& Proud". This is an upbeat show that looks at our lives as two strong bisexual business women and that any kind of relationship can work—if you want it to. I was asked how I felt about sex still being a taboo subject and yet drugs, violence and war are more acceptable to see.

My answer to this question nicely follows on from my last piece for *Polluto* called "Sex, Lies, Religion". The indoctrination of 2,000 years of religion is very hard to break. Apparently we are all born as sinners and should spend our entire life purifying ourselves, so when our time comes to leave this mortal coil we'll be pure enough to enter Heaven.

Of course, you're free to believe whatever you wish, so long as you don't believe it's okay to go to war and believe God is on your side.

If there is a God, he will be looking down in disgust at all the violence, war and poverty caused by all the greed in the world.

In comparison to war, sex isn't a sinful act. It's completely outrageous to believe it's sinful to feel content and to be dictated to as to who you should love. After all, if you are not happy in your sex life then this often leads to being aggressive, and surely God would prefer us to have sex and be happy than tear each other apart with frustration and greed.

Now onto the most popular subject in the tabloids and magazines: drugs. I'm going to name names, as I would like to think I speak for many who are sick and tired of hearing and reading about people with drug habits. We have Amy Winehouse, Pete Doherty and Kate Moss, to name a few, all grabbing our attention with crack pipes on the internet and court appearances. Do you really want these people all over front covers of magazines, airbrushed to hell to hide the drug damage, being at the forefront for your children and teenagers to look up to—to believe they're cool?

The message the press are giving, no matter how much they may slate these individuals, is that it's okay to do drugs because it can give you all the attention you need to have a successful career. In fact, why not show children and teenagers that it is rewarding to take drugs by giving Kate Moss her own clothing range? That's a great idea!

The glorification of drug taking should be stopped. The press must ignore the flavour of the month's attention-seeking habit. If the press just stopped writing about them then these individuals would have to go another route—the exploitation of their musical talent for example.

If he/she has a single or album out that week and they 'coincidentally' need to go into rehab, then erase their name from your pages until they grow up and take responsibility. The press say, 'Well they sell papers and that's what we are here to do; we are a business!' Well I would like to add that you can always run your business without people paying more than the price of the newspaper! They need to start to think of the impression this is giving to younger people who read their paper and take responsibility.

There is nothing good to come out of using drugs but there is everything to gain having sex. The mentality of adults when nudity comes on the TV towards their kids is a joke and deeply immature! A lot of adults are bringing up their children to constantly feel ashamed of what they naturally have. This can only breed insecurities within the child.

And yet, when violence is on the TV then that's ok for your child to watch? Playstation games are rife with violence. In *Grand Theft Auto* you can go with a hooker and then slit her throat to get your money back! What message is this giving out to everyone? What is this saying about girls who work in the sex industry? Yeah, some people will say it's only a game, but this can still send a damaging message to girls, saying they are worthless and lower than life. I believe that prostitution should be legalised so the girls are protected instead of wandering the streets. Maybe I'll touch on this subject in another piece in more detail.

A few months ago, my local Lush store was doing a promotion which they called 'Naked'. The promotion was to show that all their products are natural and free from excess packaging. The girls were stood outside their store wearing shorts and a long pinnie to cover their fronts, so all they were showing were their backs and legs.

The police were called and the Lush girls were told to 'cover up' or stay in the store as adults were complaining that they didn't want their children seeing them. The girls argued that they weren't doing anything wrong and yet the police told them they would be in trouble if they didn't cover up.

I love the way adults express their insecurities through their children. Children wouldn't care if the Lush girls were stood there naked! Most kids love to run around naked because they think it's fun and have no hangups about their appearance. I used to run around naked as a child and found it very liberating and would giggle my head off.

It's being fed into their heads by adults that it's wrong and dirty. But let's face it, if you think in a sordid way, then surely you are the one that needs to be mentally questioned. They're not protecting their children by making their kids feel ashamed of nudity; they are crushing them. This is why people can be so uncomfortable and frustrated with themselves as they are growing up. We have all heard of the "mummy's boy" where his mother has brought him up to believe girls are dirty and therefore he becomes very aggressive towards the opposite sex through the frustration of pleasing his mother and following his natural instincts of dating and socialising.

So, which is the most harmful? Drugs or sex? Children will naturally develop into young adults in their own time and will become naturally curious about sex as this is all part of growing up.

Drugs rot your mind and can make you paranoid and eventually dependent on them. I doesn't just rot away at your own mind and body; it also rots away at your relationships with other people. It may have given you an amazing time once, maybe twice, but you are one of the lucky ones who didn't have a bad reaction. Lots of people never get a second chance. Would you like the one you love to take that chance?

When my time comes to have a child, because I haven't ruled it out, I know how I will be guiding him or her. What they see in the mirror is nothing to be ashamed of. I will make no fuss about anybody else being nude. When they start to ask questions about sex then I will do the responsible thing and answer their questions. Why? Because I would like my child to know he or she can come and talk to me about anything—especially the boy or girl they fancy, their sexuality. I will not lose out on the growing up of my child, like many other adults do by acting embarrassed and making the child confused and suppressed with no one to turn to.

Drugs will no doubt still be in the press in years to come. Another idiot taking them, being 'caught' and then their career gets a boost from it. I will tell it as it is to my child —there is nothing glamorous about taking any kind of drug. I will show these people to my child for what they really are: a born loser who can't handle their career!

The End

Cinquain For Janet Jackson

by
Janis Butler Holm

Shock frock
on boob tube. Chest
fest. Bodice rip, sunburst
nip. O orb fantastic! Perfect,
plastic.

A Sequence Of Rashes

by
KC Wilder

#98: Essentially Romantic

Over the edge we steal

our barely liberated meat
digits arms and legs imagined
blown across black sheets

conduits for all we find absolutely necessary
entertaining hardcore visions
and the whirling twirling neon sanctity of humanism

in absentia
as our spirits shoot above the landscape
towers in a labyrinthine garden of delight

we believe in mystery
holding coiled stems of flowers

slipping from the gonzo hands of fate
our frazzled brains fall out

we blast off like rockets
what we want to do is love
before we leave this world for good

followed round by frenzied swirls of unforgiving air
like wild horses frantic
leaping into great unknowns
essentially romantic

Rash #54: Victor Zipping Into Skanky New York City Streets

for Victor Poison-Tete and Lester Bangs

a grinchly prince of rock and roll
guerilla war heroic
leaving all sur-real estate in trenchant heaps subverted
his band was named rat at rat r
with it he would cook up malto molten molotov cocktails

salient notes from his guitar
delinquent in the stratosphere
emulated frothy comics blasting submachine guns

victor zipping into skanky new york city streets
spinning off a whirling dervish style all his own
exposing his bicuspid points in an eastern seaboard way
victor unleashed prescient art

jumping headlong into crowds
deconstructing rock and roll
clamoring and inspiring dangling
no new york school wiring

Rash #97: Objects du'Fart

akhbar in a suicide belt crosses burning on his face
screaming death to infidels while waving a kalishnakov
in that fateful moment before his soul is ripped apart
he lets go a stylin' load of hippopotamus farts

floating upside down in spacesuit cosmonaut encrusted farts
farmer lands on tractor bruised up bottom keening farts

typically the fedex man
a character who looks intent arranging packages and yet
once he leaves his truck poom fart

sometimes even goldfish fart
snails and crabs fine crustaceans bilious bodies stuffed in shells
dappled by toxified phosphate leaden waters bubbling farts

vladimir putin and bob newhart
seated every evening at their dinner tables fart

even steven hawking farts
through a small electro gizmo wired to his chair
as he's wheeled before a crowd
this custom made metal box can be heard passing air

rapping up a most amazing and ingenious unique sound
flatulent saucy bean eating bono proudly belts out U fart 2

every fat american is destined to indelibly boogie
from each bottom loud slam bams like heavy field artillery
launching high into the sky
a monumental fart

Rash #1.0: Gnarley Julie

finding traces deep inside
unfamiliar places
taking stock of what surrounds
gnarley julie paces

gasket leakage fenders missing
taillights mostly cracked

trudging home from work
head still swirling feeling drained
she recharges batteries
calms herself with music

johnny cash grandmaster flash and kurt cobain
cd's plucked from cases
scratched up covered with mayonnaise

a nation of glassine
abomination office towers
keening city suburbs spinning
muy kaleidoscopic

sparks from gnarley julie's wire
flashing indications on the dashboard of desire
sable tipped mascara spear glistens up above her brow

searching for serenity
the best way she knows how
rash #26: strumming a tragic acoustic guitar

elbows on the hood of my very dinged up honda

finding myself in central rwanda
dithered and danced with the unhurried sky
opening wings like a butterfly

taking some heat in the south of sudan
thought of andorra and gypsy rose lee
stopped in helsinki christchurch and tasman
traveling silvery mountains and valleys

bent down to scribble tried to explain
slept on a steamboat got off a plane
dark situations drove me insane
entities inside of me slammed against the walls of trouble

crashed in bangkok and mumbai
speechless without knowing why
sallied on horseback dallied on foot
practicing yoga believed it was good

hurried through cities completely unknown
screwed off the mouthpiece of my telephone
picking through mottle picking through dirt
brushing unlikely debris from my shirt

staggered through denmark my final conclusion
after transcending and braving confusion
out on an island eyeing the stars
groped in the shadows of venus and mars

destiny brushes the back of my car
strumming a tragic acoustic guitar

Rash #46: Two Ultra Quirky Boats Flamingo Colored Cars

gonzo creature in a tree
disappearing suddenly
startled by this monster duo
pulling up haphazardly
two ultra quirky boats flamingo colored cars

with ineluctable energies
like luminescent shooting stars
shimmering in tandem really
two ultra quirky boats flamingo colored cars

two periwinkle substrates strewn from fat black wheels
drawing laughs like circus clowns
a twist maroon their looks and sounds
embodiments of gemini
two ultra quirky boats flamingo colored cars

two tomato nibbity nobs
strangely peeling down the highway
double ruby velvet wheels
twinkly domes of chrome and steel
flossed by silver moon and stars
two ultra quirky boats flamingo colored cars

honking unexpectedly
goosed by scarlet setting sun
twofold donkeys on a hillside fire engine crimson
all popped open for a gander
shapes that glisten from inside
two ultra quirky boats flamingo colored cars

Rash #90: What's Behind This Dicey Curtain Cutting Into Space And Time?

what's behind this dicey curtain cutting into space and time?

the living and the dead are said to mix and mingle there
at this point it well might be a comic book contention

netherworldly entities in labcoats sketching out
the teensy tiny universe of fauxbrow american poetry

Damaged

by Steve Redwood

The Library shelves were unusually well-stocked today, with golden-skinned women dangling languid bare legs over the edges. They were not allowed to speak here, of course, but their sad eyes pleaded, "Take me, take *me*." Through a half-open door at the back, he saw a couple of them being treated.

He pushed Maria 8, her skin already unhealthily blotched, towards the counter, and forced a smile for the Blueskin sitting behind it. She didn't return it.

"I've come to renew this woman," he said. His tone was defensive.

She frowned. "There'll be a renewal fee, of course."

"I know."

She took his name—John William Smith—and Social Security number, then tapped buttons on her computer keyboard, her fingers moving with the speed of hummingbird wings.

Behind her, he noticed a huge reproduction of Magritte's shrouded lovers. Were they hiding their faces from each other to avoid disappointment? he wondered.

She printed out a sheet from the computer, and passed it over to him.

He glanced at it, then looked up angrily.

"But this is twice as much as last time!"

"That is correct."

"But why?"

She looked at him through lidless eyes. "You know very well that the longer she goes without a Service the quicker she deteriorates. And the treatment is correspondingly more costly."

The computer bleeped. She glanced at it, and then looked back at him.

"It appears that someone has reserved her, anyway. For . . . let's see . . . the 14th. Next month."

"What!"

"Which means you couldn't renew her for more than two weeks anyway."

Inside, he felt an enormous relief. No more pretence! It was no longer up to him! But at the same time . . .

"Who's reserved her?"

"You know we can't give out information like that."

Maria 8 stood to one side, her face expressionless. But he could almost smell her fear.

"But I don't understand. Why does he want *her*? Was he the owner before?"

She refused to reply.

He knew it wasn't wise, but he couldn't stop himself muttering, "It's not as if she was in very good condition even when I got her!"

The Blueskin's head snapped up, and her third eye pulsed ominously.

"Please remember you are on State Benefits! We provide for your minimum sexual necessities, but you can't expect us to provide you with the latest models, or allow you to pick and choose what you think suits *you*. If you want a brand new woman, then get yourself a job, and *pay* for one!"

Realising he had gone too far, he made a placating gesture.

"I'm sorry. It's just that this bill is so much higher than I expected."

"I can't help that. Please make up your mind: do you still want to renew her—but only till the 14th—or would you rather exchange her now?"

He glanced across at Maria 8, remembered where he was, and looked quickly back at the Librarian. He hoped she hadn't noticed his weakness.

He intended to say, "Well, if it's only a couple of weeks, I might as well return her now." What he actually said was:

"My present renewal is still valid until the end of this month. Can I come back in a day or two and let you know?"

She looked surprised. Then frowned. "You can do that, if you wish."

"Yes, thank you, I think I'll do that. Goodbye."

He didn't waste time smiling this time, but, pushing Maria 8 before him, moved towards the door, trying not to notice the array of sparkling legs. Maria, his treacherous mind remarked, was like a grey cloud passing in front of the sun.

So someone had reserved her. As the unemployed were not allowed to make reservations, and the average working citizen would not be allowed to use State Benefits, it had to be somebody *above* the system. Someone really high up. He felt almost relieved. It was out of his hands. He'd done his best. She couldn't blame him for this.

But he knew she would.

Π

He sat thinking as she prepared the lunch in the kitchen. She had hardly spoken on the way home. He noticed his hands were clammy. Nervousness. But why, for God's sake? He'd done more than could ever have been expected of him. Not only renewed her twice already, but even been prepared to do it yet a third time! Which would have made four months. Four whole months with the same used woman! He doubted if anyone else in the City had ever kept a woman out as long as that without a Service, certainly not one as damaged as she had been.

Lunch was uncomfortably silent, until at last he said, trying to adopt a light tone:

"Well, it seems you have an important admirer! You should feel complimented."

"Maybe I would if I knew who it

was." A moment's silence. Then inevitably: "Why didn't you exchange me then, get it over with? Like you really wanted to?"

He didn't answer at once. A few weeks before, he would have flared up, demanded to know how she could be so ungrateful: acting the victim, when *he* was the one making the sacrifices! But he was now resigned to her distrust, knowing, deep down, that it wasn't unfounded.

Two weeks before, she had caught him glancing through the catalogues.

"I'm only *looking*!" he had protested as she stared at him with sadness and disappointment. "Come on, if I really wanted another woman, I only have to take you back, like everyone else!"

He had meant it as a defence, not a threat, but it had been a turning point. She had never mentioned it, but he knew she had never forgiven him.

Which was crazy, since there was nothing to forgive.

Now, he said, not answering her question: "It's almost better this way. For your sake, I mean. Maria, if you don't go in for a Service soon, you're going to be really ill. You could even die!"

"A Service would destroy my memories."

"But sooner or later, not having one will destroy *you*!"

"I *am* my memories."

"You lost your other memories, the ones before me, and yet you've been all right."

"All right? When I came here, I was empty, empty, *empty*! Do you want me to return to that again?"

He looked at her, wanting to say so much—and yet not enough. When she had arrived, she had been nothing more than a bright shiny receptacle for his desires. Someone who had language, and a passable knowledge of everyday things, but not a single personal memory. This had been a conscious policy decision on the part of the Government, once the Blueskins had offered their skills: it was bad enough not being able to afford to buy your own woman, without having to put up with any emotional baggage the State hand-outs might be carrying.

And he'd renewed her, and renewed her again, and his reward was that she had developed enough character and personality to be able to . . . what?

To have her own desires? To presume to *judge* him?

Before he could answer, there came a ring at the door. Voices. Steve! That was one person he would have preferred not to see right now. Especially if he had come—and he would have, of course!—with his new woman.

Maria opened the door. Steve looked at her, surprised.

"You're still here?" he said. He had no intention of being rude or hurtful.

"Nor for long," she replied,

Steve's new woman stood smiling beside him. She wasn't exactly beautiful, of course—after all, Steve too was on State Benefits—but really *glowing*. It wouldn't last very long. Within a very short time she too would begin to lose her shine. It always happened. The women always lost their shine. Nonetheless, the contrast now between the two women was too painfully marked, like the difference between a waterfall throwing back flashes of sunlight, and stagnant pond water on a grey day. And he was more than ever conscious of how *thin* Maria's skin had become, what was left of it. Almost transparent. The signs of previous operations were now clearly visible.

Also the size of the wounds she had suffered.

Who could have done a thing like that?

Steve at once steered him towards the kitchen.

"Don't tell me you've renewed her again! Whatever for?"

"I couldn't do it. I couldn't dump her back on the shelf again."

"OK, OK, we all go through this at some time or other. It's natural. We grow fond of them. Nothing wrong in that. I renewed a woman once. But this is the third time! *Look* at her, John, almost no shine left, she's already decaying. She *has* to be Serviced. You can always take her out again, if you really like her."

"She wouldn't remember me, you know that."

Steve slapped him on the shoulder. "So what? So long as she remembers how to cook and clean and treat your cock like an emperor . . . !"

He was right, of course. Few men denied that it was more pleasant if you liked the woman you rented, but it could hardly be considered indispensable.

"She's been reserved, in any case."

Steve whistled his surprise, and was about to say something when his new woman, followed by Maria, came into the kitchen, already looking anxious. They were all like that at the beginning, unable to be away from their men for more than a few minutes without something akin to panic setting in. While obviously not the same quality as those in the private sector, Steve's woman was still in very good shape, perhaps the best the Library—that was odd, why was it called a Library? he suddenly wondered—had to offer. He could have drawn her out himself the week before, he thought ruefully. W*hat's wrong with me?*

"Isn't this a lovely kitchen?" she said. Her voice was high, sharp, like a new kettle.

"It's the same as any other subsidised housing," Maria answered coldly. It was clear she didn't much like her. Didn't want to remember what she had once been herself?

"But you've made it *specially* nice, I can tell! To keep John happy. Still, you'll see, I'll do even better for Steve!"

"I applaud your ambition."

"Oh, isn't it wonderful to be off the shelves? To be alive?"

There was the tiniest pause before Maria answered: "What does 'alive' mean?"

The other woman frowned momentarily, then giggled.

"It means making Steve the happiest man in the world!"

"Ah yes. Something only you could do, of course."

Nonplussed, the woman turned her attention to Steve. John saw, however, that his friend, though holding and caressing his woman, wasn't really listening to her at all, he was listening to Maria. *Steve has noticed it, too!*

That was satisfaction of a sort. A small recompense.

The visitors didn't stay very long. Besides, it was impossible to talk to Steve in private. He would arrange to meet him later.

Afterwards, Maria said: "Steve looks very happy today. Why do you think that is?"

She was deliberately provoking him. "I don't know. You tell me." The worst possible response.

"I don't need to." She was staring out of the window. The light picked out the tendons of her muscles. 'Flayed' was the word that came to mind.

He wanted to shout out, "Well, show some appreciation, then!" but held himself in check. It didn't help.

"What are you trying to prove?"

The injustice stung.

"I'm not trying to prove anything. But, God damn it, I'm doing it for you!"

She swung round, her eyes blazing.

"Yes, for *me*! That's just it! Not for *you*! Just for me! Oh, John, don't you see, it's almost worse this way, it's almost worse!"

"What's wrong with you! What more do I have to do to . . . ?"

To . . . what? The words went round his head like an echo, like another voice.

He stormed out into the dingy back yard. She followed him a few minutes later.

"Oh John, I'm sorry, it's the memories, that's what I'm scared of losing. I'm so scared of waking up one day, and there was no yesterday."

She touched his arm, and added:

"And there are things I've learnt that I know I wouldn't learn again, not with a different man."

There were many things he could have said then. He said none of them. The moment passed.

Such moments had never come in his life before. He didn't know how to handle them.

Π

Who had reserved her? Some lover of the low life who had simply liked her photo in the catalogues, or—a chilling thought—the same man who had caused all that damage before? He was afraid of him, without knowing why. He felt—although he had no logical reason to feel this—that the reservation of Maria 8 had been a challenge to him personally. He sensed danger, as if he were a beetle lying helpless on its back on the edge of a sandpit, and the nameless man was the lion ant lurking beneath. If he struggled, the first grain of sand would start to fall in, then the second . . .

Π

Watching her undress that night, he noticed more signs of decay. Where the gold had flaked off, bruised flesh was showing through, and hair was beginning to show under her armpits, and on the lower part of her belly. As she got into bed, he noticed a slight odour. For the first time it entered his mind that she might actually die.

He cursed himself for his own weakness. Here he was, with a woman becoming more unattractive day by day—even her hair now showed streaks of brown and black—when all he had to do was exchange her, like everyone else did.

It was ridiculous, there would be no point in renewing her for two more weeks. She would simply deteriorate more. He would exchange her tomorrow. It would be the best thing for her.

He woke up in the night, and found her curled up on the floor, naked, weeping silently, photographs of their early days clutched in her thin hands, smudged with her tears.

II

He took her to the Library the following day to renew her.

The Blueskin didn't hide her displeasure.

"If you do insist on taking her out again, why don't you at least leave her overnight, so she can have a Service? She'll be ready again by midday tomorrow."

"Without any memories."

"Of course. A Service deletes personal memories, egoism, desires. That's what you brought us here for."

"No, thank you. It's only for two weeks, anyway. I'll take her as she is, if you don't mind."

She obviously did mind, but proceeded to fill out his Library card. As she was doing it, he suddenly thought: since the Services are so vital, why do they even *allow* women to be renewed without one? Why give us the choice? It didn't make sense.

A lot of things, he was beginning to realise, didn't make sense.

As they were leaving, the Librarian said:

"Remember, she must be back by the thirteenth at the latest. To allow time for Servicing. We'll repair her, of course, make her as good as new, but we can't guarantee she won't be mistreated in the future."

Why had she said that? He turned round slowly, unwillingly, while a warning voice was telling him not to listen.

"What are you saying?"

"I'm simply reminding you that there are no guarantees for the future of Maria 8."

"Why should anyone harm her?"

"That's a question we often ask. Indeed, that's why we're all here, isn't it?"

"Are you saying that this other man, the one who's reserved her, will harm her? *Has* harmed her in the past?"

"No, I'm not saying anything. I'm simply reminding you that there are no guarantees."

"But why are you telling *me*? Now?"

"It's a warning we give to all our . . . clients who keep a woman longer than is necessary or advisable. We assume that the woman has been renewed because the client is seeking more than sexual gratification. And might therefore have some interest in what happens to her after she is returned."

She paused for a moment, and he saw the triumphant malevolence in her third eye.

"I've been authorised to inform you, by the way, that the person who made the reservation was the Prime."

He turned away and walked out slowly, this time completely unaware of the glittering women on the shelves and their vacant golden eyes.

Π

The days fell away like the last leaves of autumn, fluttering away from his reach as he tried to grab and hold them.

Things changed with Maria 8. Not only because this was the final renewal, but because of the Librarian's last words, which buzzed round his head like disturbed hornets.

He told himself again and again that whatever happened to Maria 8 after the 14th, he was in no way responsible, there was nothing he could do. Yes, he might, or might not, have made the final renewal only out of a sense of guilt, or weakness, or sheer cussedness, or some incipient sense of loyalty—he didn't know himself—but he found himself worrying more and more about her future.

. . . Because he was beginning to feel certain that it was the man who had just reserved her who had inflicted the terrible wounds which were becoming more and more visible as her golden skin fell away. He had no evidence at all for this, it was as if the knowledge had always been with him.

The last traces of Maria 8's brightness disappeared. In bed, he had begun to notice a strong odour when they copulated. She had begun to sweat. Her breasts now flattened slightly when she lay down. Although he tried to continue doing the household chores as before, she was tired, and frequently didn't finish them.

There was no logical reason at all to keep her now. And every reason not to.

But he realised with shock and something akin to fear that, even so, he didn't want to take her back.

He had no word for this unknown feeling.

But it was the day he realised this that he began to wonder whether there might be some way to avoid returning her.

But for the reservation by the Prime, it might have been possible. He could have invented excuses not to return her—forgetfulness, illness, and so on—and in the end the Library might have simply let the matter pass. It could hardly matter to them, he thought, which of the women were in stock, and which were out on loan.

But you didn't mess around with the Prime. His power was absolute. He owned everything. It was said that he could annihilate you with a mere thought.

Yes, the Prime's power here was absolute. But outside the City?

All his life, there had been rumours that the City wasn't everything, that there existed somewhere else, an outside, a magical place where women didn't have to be Serviced, where the Blueskins were unknown.

But no one who left the City, it was said, ever returned.

He mentioned his crazy idea to Maria. The look she gave him then, the way she came across and folded herself in his arms, made the idea seem not crazy at all.

They made their plans.

And were arrested fifteen days later on the outskirts of the City, taken to the Palace, and hurled into separate dungeons there.

Π

After he had been lying alone for a few hours,

shivering, listening to the sinister dripping of water somewhere, a bright light suddenly burst into the cell. No one was to be seen, but a voice boomed and echoed all around him.

"John, you've surprised me. I really didn't believe we had it in us."

"What have you done with Maria?"

"Your first question is about the woman. I'm learning a lot. But I can't answer that question yet, I'm afraid."

"Who are you?"

"And I, your King, your Keeper, only merit the second question. I *could* be offended. Thing really are so much simpler here. Me, I'm the Prime, of course. And the next question is, or should be, "Who is the Prime?" However, for the sake of your sanity, I don't think I'll answer that question, either. Not yet."

"Why am I here?"

"If you mean 'here', in this cell, why, the answer's obvious. You've been a bad bad boy. But if you mean—which, of course, you didn't, but never mind—'here' as in 'in the City', why, to see what you're going to do."

"What do you mean?"

"Why do geneticists love fruit flies so much? Because they don't waste time hanging around, they live and die in a couple of weeks, things are speeded up, you can see what's really happening. The Big Picture."

"Why did you reserve Maria?"

"Hmm, the heretic interrogates the Inquisitor! This is a strange place, indeed! But I don't mind: even your questions are my answers. I just told you. To speed things up. Put you under pressure. Anyway, she isn't *your* woman. She's ours."

"Did you own her before? Was it you who damaged her?"

"Now *there* you've really hit the nail on the head! That's what I'm trying to find out. Was it *me* who damaged her? And if so, do I care? That's why I'm here. Or should I say, that's why you're here. Tell me, what were you planning to do?""

John didn't answer.

"You weren't planning to leave my little kingdom, were you?"

John remained silent.

"Ah well, I can wait, I'm not a fruit fly," the other said calmly. "Meanwhile, let's take a *really*—close peek at your mind, shall we?"

They must have drugged him, because he began to have a crazy dream, or vision, he didn't know which. He thought he saw himself asleep on a bench outside a restaurant, and Tweedledum wandered by with Tweedledee, saying to Alice, "If that there King was to wake, you'd go out—bang!—just like a candle!" Opposite the restaurant, there was a statue of an eyeless prince, the tiniest sliver of gold leaf hanging from one shoulder, with a dead bird lying at its feet—whether swallow or nightingale, he couldn't be sure, but it was well and truly dead, stiff and cold, and somehow that seemed to matter. A frog hobbled out of the restaurant on crutches, accompanied by another Prince, this time a little one, who was wearing an elephant on his head. "They ate my legs, and didn't even kiss me!" the frog muttered. "Don't they realise how vital it is to kiss me?" It swivelled a reproachful eye back inside the restaurant. "I guess, to be fair," the Little Prince was musing, "it was easier for me: I only had one rose on the planet, in any case. We're going for a stroll with Jorge in the Garden of Forking Paths," he added, "where we might well see some butterflies, very educational, their life cycle. If you'd like to join us . . . "

The vision began to dissipate. He knew he wanted to go with them, that they had the answers, but . . .

"Not just yet. One final turn of the screw, to be sure."

The voice was his own. But he hadn't spoken.

Π

He was taken to see Maria the next day. Her body lay on the floor in a corner. It was dull and heavy, a soggy, imperfect thing. There was blood between her legs.

He flung off the guards in a fury, knelt down, lifted her, and held her and howled, while his tears, the first ones he had ever shed, fell on the dull, lifeless flesh.

And where they fell new skin sizzled into existence, skin that gleamed and flashed and danced in the light, and flickered all around, swirled like trillions of tiny glistening raindrops that rapidly engulfed him.

Π

The rain poured down but still the man—whose name might or might not have been John William Smith—walked. And walked. Lines of Robert Browning echoed through his mind like the ticking of an underwater clock:

My soul

Smoothed itself out, a long-cramped scroll

Freshening and fluttering in the wind

Π

When, drenched with the rain, he finally entered the flat, he heard her in the kitchen. He threw off his coat, dried himself in the bathroom, and stood for a long time staring down into the garden. The sun broke out, and the water droplets on the leaves suddenly shone and shimmered in the light. Brighter than gold. He rubbed his eyes and frowned. As if trying to catch a memory. He went slowly downstairs and into the kitchen.

She was at the sink. Thin arms, so often holding a dishcloth or a Hoover, thin legs, so often dragging her back from the shopping, thin face, so often hardly even noticed, let alone kissed. Etiolate, because he had stopped giving her any light . . . how could anyone shine with no light?

As if in a trance, he went to her, lifted her arms out of the sink, and pulled her towards him, forcing her head against his chest, and held her.

Just held her.

He had once, years ago, had words for this feeling.

The End

Steel Teeth And Synthetics

by
Michael R. Colangelo

Jens was standing in the lineup outside the entrance to Skull and Crossbones when the twins passed by.

He could have sworn one of them winked at him, and so he stepped from his spot to follow the pair of beauties.

They could be Synths. They might be a pair of perfect traps set up by the meat merchants. But they also could be from the Hill—genetically-altered into perfection and down here looking to ensnare a different sort of meat.

It was a risk he was willing to take.

What did he care if they led him into a trap, anyway? The radiation poisoning was beginning to take its toll. All of his teeth were long gone. He had replaced them, one-by-one, with sharpened steel. But what would he replace his insides with when all his organs started to rot away? He could not afford organic replacements, and stealing hydraulics and plastics from the remnants of the military was out of the question.

He thrust his hands into the pockets of his jacket and crossed his fingers in secret. Tonight, he could get lucky. The tall and blonde twins he stalked could get him laid and might be packing some expensive artificial parts beneath their creamy skin. Or, they might be hunter droids, and they would kill him.

Dead or alive, though, he couldn't really lose.

Not really.

He caught a glimpse of platinum blonde hair turning down an alleyway off Port

Street. He paused at the mouth of the trash-strewn alley and listened to the click of their stiletto heels fade.

For courage, he took a glass capsule from beneath his coat, broke it, and then snorted its contents. The familiar rush of Dust filled his senses. With it came the old feelings of invulnerability and superhuman strength. Once he was satisfied in the knowledge he could no longer be harmed, he followed them down the alleyway.

Their journey ended before a steel garage door set into the side of an abandoned factory. One of them knocked, and the corrugated steel opened just high enough for the pair to duck beneath. When they passed, the door came down again, and Jens found himself alone in the alley.

He approached the door and hesitated only for a moment before knocking himself. The Dust was pumping at full strength through his veins. If they wouldn't let him inside, the drug made him feel like he might be able to punch through the steel door, regardless.

But the door lifted, as it had for the twins, and he ducked inside.

It was darker inside than the alleyway had been. He paused for a moment to let his eyes adjust. The interior was packed with people. Some were milling about, but most of the crowd were focused on a large stainless steel stage set in the center of the open factory space.

He quickly took mental note of some of the crowd: the twins he had followed, a group of men in dark sunglasses and equally dark suits, a pair of girls with neon-green hair who didn't look a day over twelve-years-old, and a very large black man whose hydraulic arm and leg joints gave away his true nature.

He mingled with the crowd and continued taking notes. Everyone gathered had some sort of modification. That meant they had money, or were owned by someone who had money. The pit of his stomach began to sink heavy with an icy feeling. The rich were not inclusive and pretty dangerous towards outsiders. The trend was to consider anyone who lived outside the Hill as slaves, thrill kills, or food.

He shrugged off the feeling. As long as he kept to himself, nobody could possibly realize he didn't belong.

He found a dark corner and took out his cell phone. It was old technology, but it still worked fines if other phones were rigged to match the same frequency. He called Jean-Charles.

"Hello."

"You'll never guess where I'm standing," he whispered.

"You are outside my window, naked with a birthday cake in hand, perhaps?"

"Almost as good."

"Will you tell me one day, little Jens? I am terribly busy." Jean-Charles sighed.

He could hear a woman screaming in the background.

"Look. I've just found a bunch of Synths having some kind of party. You need to get down here with some of your men."

"You are inside the Hill?"

"That's the best part. They're out here in Badtown."

"Doing what?"

The stage lit up with an array of bright strobe and floodlights and the crowd applauded. A well-dressed Asian man in a pin-striped suit took the stage. He made his way to a podium at the front as the crowd roared its approval.

"I don't know!" Jens hollered into the phone. "I'm about to find out! Come down to Skull and Crossbones and I'll meet you there!"

He hung up the phone.

Whatever was about to happen, the crowd was lit up over it. Their excitement, combined with the drugs in his system, made Jens feel lit up too.

While the Asian man fiddled with the podium, something was wheeled in overhead on the big rails bolted to the factory ceiling. It was an enormous torpedo-shaped unit made of steel with a screen affixed to its front. Optic cabling and wires hung haphazardly from its sides, and huge sheets of vacuum plastic protected the machinery from the dust and pollution hanging in the air.

The screen flickered twice, accompanied by a loud humming sound, and then flashed to life. The screen bathed the interior of the factory in a sickly green light. Overhead, a giant green eye surveyed the proceedings below it.

"Ao is activated," the Asian man announced into a microphone. He let the crowd roar for a few moments longer before motioning with his hands for them to be quiet. The factory settled into a steady thrum of hushed and whispered voices. Somebody coughed close to where Jens was standing.

"In order to provide proper worship towards our Imperial Majesty, we have a special surprise for you this evening."

He motioned off-stage to a group of men milling near a parked ambulance, long stripped of its Old City markings. At the front of the stage, a pair of women were setting up a length of table covered with a Koi-patterned tablecloth. They set out steel cooking bowls and glass condiment jars and stacks of Styrofoam plates.

The men wheeled a gurney from the back of the ambulance. Strapped to it was a young, squirming, and naked girl. The crowd erupted again when they saw her. The eye on the ceiling looked down impassively.

He had seen human sacrifice before. Many times at the old Mahomet Gentleman's Club when live snuff shows were big and they'd opened their doors to the public temporarily. It wasn't the sacrifice that bothered him, however, it was the set up. A bunch of rich artificials were congregating in Badtown, and it appeared as if they had built a giant computerized eye to worship as some kind of god.

The crowd was lining up in single file on either side of the stage, and the women from the buffet table were moving through the rows handing out knives and forks. A wave of ice washed over him as he realized what they were preparing to do to the poor girl strapped down on stage.

He felt severely out of place, and he could suddenly no longer look at the eye hanging from the ceiling for fear that it would meet his gaze.

He backed away from the stage towards the garage doors and briefly considered calling Jean-Charles and telling him not to bother. These artificials weren't some misguided group of rich Hill dwellers playing at satanic worship. No, there was something much more serious going on.

If he cancelled on Jean-Charles though, it would only anger him, and Jean-Charles would have no qualms with scavenging him and selling him to the butchers at the square in a fit of irritation.

He found the winch that opened the doors and pulled on it until the doors lifted just high enough so he could duck beneath them.

Outside, the cool night air felt good

on his skin. The garbage smell of Badtown felt good too. The girl on stage began to scream and he scurried away as the doors slammed shut again behind him. He hurried along the alleyway and back through the crowded street towards Skull and Crossbones.

The lineup had not thinned. In fact, in his absence, the line had stretched across the side of the building and across the street. Pedestrians blocked the road, ignoring the blaring horns of the automated transport sleds and taxi pods they held up in the intersection. Some would-be club goers had decided early they were not getting into the club, and had taken to drinking, fighting, and fucking in the street instead.

Jean-Charles was parked out in front of the club in a paint-stripped pickup truck. He sat in the passenger seat smoking a cigar with a high-powered shotgun cradled in his oversized lap. Beside him was a young and girlish-looking man in a black turtleneck. His latest muse, apparently.

Three guys sat in the back of the pickup among an assortment of power tools and ammunition. Jean-Charles saw Jens from across the street and waved him over. The grin on his jowled face was more predatory than friendly.

"Late again. I don't know if I should meet you any more."

"You want spare parts or not?"

Jean-Charles nodded.

"You pay me up front and I'll take you over there. I don't get blood on my hands, either."

"What is your price?"

"I get my pick of whatever you harvest... and five grams of Dust."

Jean-Charles rummaged through his pockets and produced a small and darkened medicine bottle. He dropped it into Jens' open palm.

"We follow you in the truck."

He took them to the entrance of the alleyway and they had trouble maneuvering with their vehicle. The streets were crawling with people who did not obey the laws of traffic. They crossed where there were no crosswalks and loitered in the center of the road. Most of these people were armed, and it was dangerous to attempt to move them along for fear of reprisal. It took them almost a full hour to reach the abandoned factory.

They parked at the mouth of the alleyway and Jean-Charles and his men stepped out of the truck, all except the river who waited behind the wheel with the engine running.

"Hold it." He told them. "You can't just walk in there. There are too many, trust me."

"That is a lot of salvage for us. The longer you stall us, the less salvage we get as they run back to the Hill."

"It's a bad idea. There are four of you."

As greedy as Jean-Charles was, he seemed to trust Jens to a degree. The pair had made some money in the past, and neither one had sold the other to rival dealers or salvagers yet. As much as Jens could see that it annoyed him, he still backed off with a flourish of dramatic exasperation.

"Fine. We wait. We hit them when they come out."

They waited for an hour and Jean-Charles passed the time in the cab of his truck with his boy-thing, while the other three stood and stared at Jens with blank, Dust-ravaged eyes. He told them jokes and stories, digging deep into his repertoire to keep their minds engaged so they didn't rough him up for kicks out of sheer boredom. He survived the hour intact, but not once did any of Jean-Charles's men crack a smile.

Their wait was over when they heard the familiar sound of clicking heels on concrete.

Jean-Charles practically leapt from the truck with his shotgun and ambled down the alleyway towards the twins that Jens had followed earlier that evening.

His men threw away their cigarette butts and followed after their boss, shoving Jens and his joke-telling aside in favor of more interesting sport.

It was over quickly.

He watched things unfold against the alleyway wall. His arms folded across his chest.

\#

When the pair was dead, they loaded them into the back of the pickup. Jean-Charles offered Jens a lift.

He rode in the back and examined the dead girls sprawled naked upon the clear plastic sheet.

In death, both had turned extremely pale. They looked artificial in their perfection. Their pale bodies were patterned with splotchy violet bruises and splashes of red crimson where they'd been split open ever so professionally. He was almost tempted enough to remove his glove to touch their skin.

He hesitated however. The other men that rode with him in the back of the truck might not understand his desire, and he had no intention of testing their open-mindedness.

They drove back through Badtown at an excruciatingly slow pace. At one point, the truck had to be stopped, and some revelers were menaced with Jean-Charles's shotgun.

When the morning sun was up, they pulled into the compound. The sun filtered through the green-black haze of pollution that hovered over the city.

Immediately following the corporate civil wars, Jean-Charles had squatted on a chain of abandoned chemical factories. There were twenty six buildings in total – old storage vats had been converted to add to his list of suitable living spaces. Here, Jens lived with about sixty other people. Jean-Charles often spoke of creating a new city that would one day overtake the old city, and while Jens didn't quite believe him, it was a good place to live in terms of protection, nonetheless. It was secure. Every year, a swarm of raiders might attempt to invade, but the compound's fortifications, manpower, and firepower always turned them away with minimal casualties and structural damage.

The vehicle stopped before a cylindrical building that was spray painted so fearsomely with graffiti that the original paint finish was completely obscured. Jens tapped on the cab window.

"I'm not going home. First pick. Remember our deal?"

The truck lurched away so quickly that it left rubber marks on the pavement and almost dumped him from the truck.

They took the bodies to a long and low building near the border of the compound. It ran alongside an electric fence and was made almost entirely of corrugated tin. Jean-Charles's reasoning was the most valuable of his salvaging equipment should be hidden in the most derelict-looking building on the grounds. It confused the raiders, and it confused any would-be thieves that might be living on the inside.

The salvage garage was set up like an old automotive repair garage. And whenever they acquired vehicles and robots, it worked in a very similar fashion.

But there were obvious differences -- racks of surgical tools and a pair of operating tables attested to a different sort of salvaging altogether. An ample industrial freezer also attested to the fact that they stored more than car parts inside the garage.

They placed the dead women on the surgical tables and Jean-Charles even did one himself. Jens loitered near the garage doors and smoked the cigarettes he'd pilfered off a countertop spread with tools.

When they were done with their butchery, Jean-Charles motioned for him to come over and take his pick.

They'd placed the good pieces on a set of large tarp coverings. Bones, meat, and anything that wasn't artificial went inside big plastic bins for grinding and freezing later on. The tripe would be sold to butchers, or it would be saved and eaten by the compound residents themselves.

The twins had been loaded with parts: a pair of hydraulic hearts, an artificial digestive system, synthetic livers, and hundreds of stainless steel joint and bone reinforcements. Jens picked out the two hearts and the digestive system. As badly as he wanted a liver, he knew that Jean-Charles would be unwilling to give them up. He saw the way that his eyes shined when he looked at those parts in particular.

Despite their deal, Jean-Charles could renege on his good nature at any point in time, and that meant that Jens would be dead if he didn't pick correctly.

They packed his items inside a clear plastic case and didn't offer to drive him back to his building. He collected his prizes and slung the case across his back. He was content enough to walk back. He would sleep through the day and night, and in the morning, he would search for a cheap surgeon who would replace his bad organs with these ones.

He got back to his place and picked the rusting lock with his picks. He'd long ago thrown away the actual key. If a door had a key, then someone could take that key. It was better to make everyone break in, all of the time.

Once he was past his front door, he turned off the alarm system he'd modified with a spring-loaded spike trap. Anyone setting off the motion detector would be faced with a cloud of iron shrapnel, propelled down the hallway from his inner foyer by a series of steam-and-motion powered propulsion engines he'd disguised as antique industrial art sculptures.

He turned on the nightlight beside his bed mattress and placed the organs inside his refrigerator, then he flipped the switch on an old laptop he was amazed to discover still worked after finding it while scouring for parts on the Scrapheap.

He took off all of his clothes and then collapsed in a heap on his old mattress, positioning the laptop at the foot of his bed so he could read it.

For the last three months, when the radiation storms had been so bad that he couldn't go outside, he'd spent all of his times reading the collected works of Isaac Asimov on the machine's decaying hard drive. The files were badly formatted and incomplete, but he found that it passed the time. He laughed often at the author's upbeat outlook of the future and wondered what Asimov might have thought of AI and robot intelligence if he'd glimpsed the feast in Badtown earlier in the night.

He fell asleep shortly afterwards and dreamed of a coastline unmarred by crashed fuel tankers and long stretches of glass beach, melted so by the nuclear heat unleashed in the wars at the start of the millennium. There was peace in sleep. It was something he missed in reality.

In the morning, he woke and ate a can of dog food. He sat in a chair and read a bit more Asimov while listening to Jean-Charles's weather and news reports on his ham radio. As sociopathic as Jean-Charles could be, everyone needed a hobby. Jean-Charles's hobby was radio broadcasting, apparently. He was a weatherman or something, before the television networks had fallen early in the wars.

When he was finished with the Asimov, he dressed and bathed in a bucket of clean water he kept near his door. He checked on the organs quickly before making his way outside with the intention of finding a doctor in the Badtown core willing to operate.

The tram platform was deserted when he arrived. Hardly anyone bothered with the city's crumbling transportation system anymore. Despite the fact that it was safer than walking or driving, especially through the contamination zones, other passengers on the tram could often be more hazardous to one's health than the environment it skipped along overtop of.

He waited on the windy platform for over an hour for the tram to arrive. It screeched along its greased cable before rattling to a grinding halt between the station platforms. Only one of its many doors slid open, and he hopped inside as a pleasant-sounding woman's voice announced long-vaporized destination points. He sat on one of the hard metal seats near the back of the tram and waited another hour before the car finally began to move again.

As the tram moved, he stared out the window and counted the alternating bands of green and yellow-hued smog haze in the horizon.

When it reached the Badtown station, Jens stepped onto the platform. A trio of tribe raiders – savages with no allegiances to any of the major factions – were already there. Two of them stood over the corpse of a dog while a third sliced the dead animal to ribbons with an army knife.

All three of them looked up at him as he exited from the tram and he froze.

The general rule of thumb in savage culture was that live meat was better than dead meat, and human meat was better than dog meat. The only weapon he carried were his teeth, and he didn't think they'd be enough if these fellows decided to act on their general preferences. They only place he could run was back onto the tram car, and that was hardly an escape. The enclosure was more of a mobile dead end than anything else.

The one with the knife snarled at him. "Anything caught in Badtown during daylight hours belongs to us."

Jens nodded.

"I'm aware. I'm just looking to barter some goods."

He motioned towards the dead escalator at the other end of the platform.

"Get lost."

He hurried past them, initially confused as to why they'd let him go. When he spotted a dog leash around the dead animal's neck as he passed, he saw that a severed hand still clutched at the leash. They'd already caught someone. His timing couldn't have been better.

During the day, Badtown was deserted. Nobody wanted to be caught in savage territory when the clubs were closed. Anybody caught moving during the day would probably be eaten or butchered for later sale or trade. He moved quickly through the empty streets.

There was an old shopping mall on the edge of Badtown that still retained some businesses. There was a Dust laboratory located on one floor, an old sporting goods outlet had been converted into an arms dealer's lair, and, his old contact, The Soviet had converted a storage space in the basement into a surgical facility.

Most of the people that Jens knew wouldn't deal with the Soviet, including Jean-Charles. It was rumored that before the Soviet came to Badtown, he peddled children along the desert border. Some even claimed that he wasn't a real doctor. But he had done Jens' mouth without complication, and that was all Jens required of him, disreputable past or not.

Two savages guarded the doors to the basement of the mall. At first, Jens thought they might have been raiding the Soviet, but the pair gave no indication of aggression when they spotted him. They opened the double steel doors behind them and gestured him through, and he hurried past them without incident.

The storage room was dark except for a single surgical light affixed to a pole. Only a single table and the Soviet himself were illuminated in the light. He was cutting a body on top of the table to ribbons and dropping pieces into a pair of buckets on the floor beside him.

He looked up from his work when Jens entered and snapped off a pair of latex gloves.

"You've returned for more work, I hope?"

Jens motioned towards the dissection on the table.

"If you're busy, I can wait."

"Oh, this is just a little fun. It passes the time."

Jens followed the Soviet's eyes to an IV drip and a heart monitor that sat beside the operating table. Whatever was left of the unfortunate, it was still alive. He fought to keep his breakfast down.

"Yes, I need some work. Heavy work this time, and a trade."

The Soviet leaned into the darkness and snapped on a light. The halogens hummed overhead and the room was illuminated in a pale yellow light. He removed his headgear and operating smock and motioned for Jens to sit at a wooden desk in the corner. Sitting across from him, the Soviet lit a cigarette and offered one to Jens. He declined politely.

"So?" The Soviet asked.

"I've a heart and a digestive tract I need installed. I have a heart for trade, too."

"Two hearts." Muttered the Soviet. Jens could see him calculating the price in his mind. Eventually, the doctor reached into his pocket and pulled out a pager. He pressed a button and the face of the device lit with a green and rapidly-blinking light.

"What's that?"

"I modified this to work within the confines of the mall. If I need something brought to me, it will be brought to me."

The doors of the operating room swung inward, and three savages stood armed with a baseball bat, a hatchet, and a pump-action sports shotgun with the price tag still attached.

Jens leaped from his chair as if it was electrified.

The Soviet was standing too. He moved away from Jens.

"I received a message this morning that some of my clients were accosted in Badtown. They were butchered for parts and my contacts inside the Hill are very displeased. Personally, I am fairly disappointed in you, Jens."

While the savage with the shotgun trained it on him, the other two closed in. He back away until his head cracked against the concrete wall of the room.

"Let's talk about this. I've got the parts but they're not on me. I know who did it too. It wasn't me."

"We know who did this too. A-O is online now, remember? A-O sees all things."

The Soviet moved to the exit of the room and shut the door behind him.

He left Jens with no choice but to fight.

#

It was tricky fighting three juiced-up and well-armed savages when all one has is a pair of sharpened steel teeth. The odds were not in his favor, and as the pair descended on him he wished he'd taken a hit of Dust prior to speaking with the Soviet. Dust made you feel less and react more.

This was going to hurt if it didn't outright kill him.

The one with the hatchet feigned a

swing and then immediately came in for a tackle. Jens caught him beneath the arms to pin the hatchet and took the savage's head in his stomach. His breath vanished in a whoosh of air and pain, and the savage drove him into the concrete wall spine-first. The force of his impact brought drywall down from the ceiling above them.

The one with the baseball bat took a swing and the wood cracked off his shoulder. Jens grimaced and then concentrated on the back of the bare neck caught at his waist. He bent over, opened his mouth, and then dug in with his teeth.

As the taste of warm blood filled his mouth, the savage grunted in pain. He bit down harder, trying to make his teeth click together through the back of his opponent's mouth. The grunt turned to a whine of pain. Jens was smashed against the wall again in panic, and his teeth were ripped free. The savage released his hold, but Jens lunged forward again with his mouth opened wide.

This time he caught the man in the face. The steel in his mouth tore through the savage's face and Jens wrapped his arms around the back of the man's head to keep him from struggling loose.

The baseball bat came down on his back again and again during their grapple, until it finally him something important and pain exploded both ways up and down his spine. The shock of the blow forced him to break his hold.

He spun away from another swing, the tip of the bat caught the curls in his hair. The shotgun went off with a deafening blast and the stinging pain of buckshot crawled up his shins. He fell over, but so did his opponent. The man's lower half was completely obliterated by the shotgun blast meant for Jens. His mouth opened and closed like frog, spewing clots of blood, brain-dead before his top-half hit the floor.

Jens grabbed the baseball bat and flung it at the man with the shotgun. He followed through with a rush, ignoring the screaming pain that made his legs tremble and sway dangerously beneath him. The bat caught the man across the hands and he fumbled the weapon. A second blast discharged harmlessly into the concrete floor.

Jens bit him across the throat and tore a huge piece of windpipe loose. He pushed the man away from him with his hands. The savage gasped for breath and fell.

Jens spit the meat on the floor and wiped his mouth with the back of his jacket.

He watched the only man still standing drag the hatchet from the floor. His mangled face had been reduced to a pair of wild eyes lost in a sea of crimson.

Jens moved towards him and the savage raised his arms in a gesture of defeat.

"No more."

Jens crushed his throat with a hard kick and watched him die slowly, struggling to breathe.

He took the shotgun and the baseball bat with him. The hatchet was awkward and heavy, and ugly besides. As he moved around the room and plucked items from the floor, the adrenaline rush from the fight dissipated and the wounds he sustained became more and more apparent.

His legs felt like they were crawling with fire ants. His back and neck felt as if the bones had been wrenched free of the connective tissue, and they probably had been. His mouth tasted foul and salty, and he wished for clean water so he might rinse the blood from it.

He wanted to steal the equipment in the room. He knew the Soviet kept spare organs and drugs somewhere, but he didn't want to delay his departure any longer than he had to. The Soviet might have had more savages on his payroll, and if he was involved somehow in what Jens had witnessed the night before, Jens didn't want any part of him or his operations anymore. He did, of course, want to find the Soviet and perhaps eat him slowly from the feet up, but that would need to wait for a better time.

For now, he needed to escape.

He limped from the Soviet's operating room and made his way back through the shopping mall. There was a group of savages milling about the parking lot when he got outside, but he managed to stay out of sight. He didn't know if they were associates of the Soviet or not. It was better he just avoided everyone until he made it back to the compound.

He didn't bother with the tram. Instead, he took the long way home back through a series of underground tunnels once used to house shops and restaurants where he could easily avoid anyone he encountered.

He made it back safely, and hurried to his quarters where he dressed his wounds, listened to Jean-Charles's afternoon weather report, and plotted his next move.

They would no doubt be looking for him now. The Soviet would tip them off to his whereabouts and they would probably come for him.

He was still contemplating his very limited options when the outside of the chemical vat was rocked with an explosion. Whatever had gone off was hot enough to feel through the thick walls. The room shuddered and his bookshelf tipped, spilling old books across the thin carpeting.

Mumbling, he put his pants back on, took up the shotgun, and went outside to see what was going on.

Somebody had driven a vintage tank through the fence at the front of the compound. Through a cloud of black oil smoke, he could see it firing shells on the cluster of towers that housed the compound residents.

Jean-Charles's men had responded quickly to the intrusion and lay on a cracked landing strip firing at the vehicle with an assortment of rifles. The bullets weren't working particularly well. Savages didn't have access to this kind of firepower. It was either the Soviet, or one of his masters from the Hill.

The tank swiveled its turret briefly and launched a shell into the midst of the compound defenders. Through the fire and exploding tarmac, Jens could hear them screaming as they burned beneath a torrent of white napalm. His stomach churned and twisted itself into a black knot. This was his fault, entirely.

The tank turned its cannon back on the housing buildings, and he ran inside. He grabbed the organ case from the refrigerator, but as he was coming back down the hallway, another shell hit his home and shook the foundations so hard that the force knocked him to the floor.

He was bathed in a heat so powerful that it singed his eyebrows and set fire to his books. The books, bookshelf, and carpet all burst into flames like dry pines in a forest fire. The ceiling in front of him caved with a shower of cinders, clouds of pulverized drywall, and broken support timbers. He scurried away from the collapsing roof and barely avoided being crushed by the fiery debris.

He scurried about the room like a trapped rat and cursed the design of his living quarters loudly. There was only one way in and one way out, and that way was currently collapsing in flames - so much for "safe" fortification.

His body shook and sweat in the heat. He smelled bad when he sweated, like a dead body. It was a side effect of the radiation poisoning, a slow decline from a man into a rotting corpse. He covered his nose and mouth with the collar of his jacket and then, clutching the box of organs tightly to his chest, rushed headlong into the fire.

He was instantly blinded and choked by the thick black smoke that filled the hallway. In his blindness and discomfort, he tripped over something and fell forward. The organs fell from his grasp and the box split open. Slush, blood, and the organs themselves spilled out across the floor. He watched the rubber nerve tip attachments that covered the objects wither and melt away beneath the heat.

They were ruined. Even if he could replace the attachments, the intense heat had already damaged the fragile alloys that composed most of the organs, warping them at microscopic levels into uselessness.

There was no time to lament his loss. The ceiling was still coming down in flaming chunks of dangerous structure. He leaped to his feet, wrapped himself in his jacket, and ran into the flames towards the unseen door.

The heat was unbearable. He could smell his hair burning and his flesh sizzling. He stumbled through the burning front door and fell to the concrete outside. His clothes were smoking and he did his best to pat out flare-ups that roiled across his body and atop his head. His skin had turned bright red like the carapace of a lobster.

The tank was rolling now. It was moving away from the cluster of burning housing buildings towards Jean-Charles's garage. Most of the compound's residents were fleeing through the opening in the fence made by the vehicle. The thick plumes of black smoke that rose into the sky reminded Jens of smoke signals. It would only be a matter of time before various savage raiding gangs saw the smoke and were attracted to it like sharks.

Jean-Charles's perverse utopia was finished. Jens huddled on the ground and tried to suppress the hot pain emanating from his burned body. He felt like a piece of barbecue charcoal.

The tank arrived at the salvage garage and kept right on going through it. The tin sides of the building collapsed and were crushed beneath the tank's treads as if the structure was made of construction paper.

Jens got to his feet and limped through the hole in the gate. He pushed his way through the crowd and veered off the main road between a pair of factories.

The savages would be on their way, and the throng of panicked residents were like a heard of scared sheep - free meat for the wolves.

He paused against the building wall to catch his breath and his cell phone began to ring.

"Hello."

"Little Jens," said Jean-Charles through the receiver. His voice was low and filled with menace. "We have hit a problem."

"Don't blame me for this. I didn't send them."

"Your mouth continues to flap, but perhaps for not much longer."

"You think I wanted this? You think I set this up somehow?"

"I do not really care of your intentions or motivations. I simply wanted – "

Jens hung up the phone, and when it began to ring again, seconds later, he threw it on the ground.

He could run, but when he was too tired to run anymore, someone would be there to catch him. He'd lost.

A pack of savages rounded the corner of the alleyway, no doubt attracted to the sound of his ringing phone. He tried to count their numbers, but his tired mind failed him, and the group blurred together in a haze of danger.

He picked up a bent and rusted iron rod from the alleyway floor – a stupid, pointless weapon to defend a stupid, pointless existence.

As the pack closed in on him, he crushed the cell phone beneath the charred heel of his boot.

And he began to laugh.

The Day She Melted

by
Frank Burton

The day she melted, she was shouting about how she's told me a thousand times, and I was shouting back telling her not to shout, when I noticed the dribbles of liquid flesh pouring down her face. She was in such a rage she barely even noticed, and it wasn't long before she became just a puddle at my feet, leaving me no choice but to weep giant Alice tears until I melted too, mixing with her molten form into one sweet swirling mass. We ran down the stairs, out the front door and down the street, waving at passers by as we rushed towards the bottom of the hill with no idea where we were going from here, but at least we were free.

Live Without A Net: Bloodletting The Robot

by RC Edrington

'This may prick just a bit.' Her voice like steel wool raping a rusted tailpipe. Her breath stale coffee and peppermint gum tinged with top-shelf vodka. She is in my face like some sickly aunt I only pretend to like so my birthday check still arrives . . . and that check is always good for a 1/2 gram of uncut Mexican Chiva.

She is scared of me, despite the liquid bravado she sips on her 'coffee' break. I sense it. Not because I am 6'2" and 230 lbs. But because I am 6'2", 230 lbs., and she is checking my blood level to ensure the various psychotropic drugs coursing through my veins are at a therapeutic level. If not, I imagine she has visions of me ripping her throat out and licking the blood as it drips in slow motion down her saggy 50-year old tits. Her B-movie fantasy, not mine—so ignore the clichéd prose.

I long ago faced the fact that this nurse, people in general, and you dearest reader, consider me crazy. But in this society I am not too certain crazy is all that bad a place to be. In fact, I often find the most logical response to reality is quite simply to go insane.

Her wrinkled hand of red finger-nails and the obligatory wedding ring shakes just a bit as she rubs alcohol along a vein on my forehead (years of heroin usage makes it impossible to fish up a sunken vein anywhere else). 'Relax,' I tell her, 'I get my blood drawn every three months. No big deal. Get it over with. Just stick the butterfly in already so I can get the fuck out of here.'

Yes, I am the crazy one. Aren't I? Think about it. This nurse, three to four times an hour, eight hours a day, five days a week, fifty-two weeks a year, for around thirty years of her life., has or will be saying: 'This may prick just a bit,' then sticks a needle in some patient's arm to suck blood. Ignore the sexual undertones. Ignore the fact her syringe takes, while my junkie spike gives. Focus on an entire lifetime doing one thing over and over and over.

The main theory among shrinks in regards to 'crazy' people (not that we are really considered people, but are treated more like robots out of some Philip K. Dick novel, which in and of itself is most likely a poor analogy given that Dick's robots are often more human than human) is to get them into a routine. It makes them feel comfortable and confident about what they are doing from one moment to the next. More importantly, it eliminates the individual's need to think. It is training people to live the life of a junkie, but replacing the euphoric rush of dope with some mundane task designed to erase time in eight-hour increments. Erasing time is a good thing. In fact, it is probably the only purpose for your or my existence.

I have accepted this. Why I am not only permitted but encouraged to slip off into a heroin-induced coma is beyond my comprehension, as are most convoluted beliefs or theories bordering on religion that propagate within your society. According to the shrinksperts, people begin to run into trouble and act crazy when they tend to think outside the mainstream or the 'norm'. Normal is boring. Normal is fucking a crack whore missionary-style in the backseat of a middle-class sedan as some bored housewife forgets about her meaningless existence at bingo.

But no dearest reader, I am not crazy—but I can certainly see why I would be viewed as such by people like yourself. You are so caught up in your daily routines that any idea or action which does not fit into the hermetically sealed program of the machine you are a cog in must be some kind of error or bug that needs to be fixed—or eliminated. But of course self elimination through heroin abuse is frowned upon. Seems the machine much prefers I suffer more slowly, one moment at a time, engaged in meaningless activities. Rest assured, however, the people who spend their life trying to fix people like myself are in much more need of being fixed than anyone.

After drawing four small vials of blood from my limp vein, she smiles like some fucked up clown tripping on LSD—serious here kids, the make-up is strictly circa 1980 pastels with reddish ballons smeared across the cheeks of a much-too-white foundation, and eye shadow like baby blue clouds rising into slick black painted on eyebrows. She slaps a tiny band-aid on my wrist and labels the vials with my name. Misspelled as per her usual bored attention to detail.

The End

After Hollywood

by
RC Edrington

She was a rich wanna-be hip bitch
from NY City
and came with an art degree,
a flare for the Orient
and an ass that till this day leaves me
dreaming of peaches and plums.
She thought it cool that I wrote,
shot too much dope
and lived in a renovated garage
with no bathroom
in the middle of an arts district
I never cared existed.

It was Summer.
But it is always Summer
in Tucson, Arizona.
The heat hung in the air
like sheets of cellophane
ready to smother us in our own juices,
while June and July fired their rounds
of endless days at me one by one.
But I ignored their flesh wounds of boredom
and restless anticipation
by keeping my mind and nerves sheltered
with the bullet proof effectiveness
of cheap whiskey, marijuana
and various other chemicals
designed to numb the soul.

It was the days that haunted me.
Time itself.
Not the faceless college summer school idiots
who roamed the downtown coffee houses
with their anal retentive textbooks
and girlfriends.
They left me alone, slumped
against an alley wall
in the shadow of a black leather jacket.

The rich bitch from NY City
called herself Sasha, not quite certain
if she sought the sophistication of the French
or the mystic romanticism of the Japanese.
By day she prayed for rain
or spent hours masturbating
with plaster in a downtown storefront
with two other pre-lesbian sculptresses
who sat around sipping designer tea
and talking like wind-up dolls
about the pain of being female
artists in a world dominated by cocks
and decadent leather kings
in snakeskin boots

So I stayed hidden
behind my notebooks
compiling a list of old friends
who stained the dingy white walls of no-tell
motels
with their pomegranate brain cells,
or accepted death more quietly
in some damp alley
where spent meat soaks in cheap whiskey
coughed up by suicidal balladeers
disguised as bag ladies,
with a rusty spike dangling
from their frail post-teenage arms.

And Sasha continued to play artist
while I continued to play house...
and that plaster aborted orgasm
she called art
had people giggling behind her back
while they assured her she was a true artist
like all of them,

and should continue to keep daddy's check
coming to the gallery.
I had stopped hanging out.
Spent day and night writing,
listening to Ziggy stardust and old X records,
and slamming the best dope
her daddy's money could buy.

We continued to fuck,
but found it increasingly impossible
to talk or even look at each other
outside of the bedroom.
Mainly because I refused
to have some Japanese dragon tattooed
on my shoulder
like all the hip new wave artists
in the New York of her dreams wore.
Or maybe it was the way the chopsticks fell
like smacked out dancers between my fingers
and I had to eat that greasy Chinese food
she was always ordering with a spoon.

Granted I had no culture,
but who really needed culture
when I had plenty of stories
tucked inside my notebooks...
like the death rock goth chick from Tempe,
Arizona
who begged I rape her in a graveyard
so she could fantasize my sperm were
maggots
and she was a corpse,
which is why she wore black lipstick
and fingernail polish...
white pancake makeup
and a 1920s wedding gown, saying
she loved heroin for the uncertainty
of not knowing which dose
would be her last dose,
She was 19, and in all her misery
she seemed much more happier than I.
We spent a few weeks together
faking suicidal tendencies
and planning our gothic deaths
like punk rock Romeo and Juliet...
questioning my sanity

and trying to convince her
the only thing I kill is time.

I left Sasha.
I guess it was August
when Shane finally surfaced
asking where I had been the past few months,
updating me on rumors of my death
and telling me about this New York artist
he was fucking...
who bought him a new guitar,
and then he flashed me the Japanese dragon
she had paid $200
to have tattooed on his shoulder...
and we laughed
like we once had laughed
when we were 17
and playing punk rock hide and seek
on Hollywood boulevard.
Before we became whores and junkies.
Before we left our souls screaming rape
beneath neon signs or in unlit alleys.
Before we scarred our minds and bodies
with cheap tattoos and razor blades.
Before, when death
was still an unfamiliar stranger
we only caught glimpses of
out of the corners of our mind...
and before I knew it
Shane too was gone.

And I know now
my life can never be
some well scripted fairy tale,
but I don't want to die
on some dirty boulevard
or spend my days
writing epitaphs in notebooks.
And I guess I have always known
I'll never be abel to lose or find myself
in the domestic rhythm
of wife-children-job
so I guess
I am just left to wander
until I can figure out
what this wandering is for.

On the Cover Artist:

Oliver Dominguez

I was born and raised in Miami, FL and have a Colombian background. Since I was a child I sought self-expression through art.

I am always intrigued by different media. Everyday I search for inspirations, motivations and influences that can make me a better artist. I am especially intrigued by Mr. Norman Rockwell, whose art has not only guided me in finding my artistic signature but also helped me in my work. Other sources of inspiration include the American Illustration masters like Howard Pyle, Norman Rockwell, and N.C. Wyeth.

I studied at the Ringling School of Art and Design and believe this provided a great starting point to my career as an editorial illustrator.

CONTRIBUTORS

KC Wilder is an artist, poet, free-speech activist, and musician. His journalism, fiction and poetry have appeared in over a thousand publications around the world.

His art and writings have appeared in *The Seattle Review, Poetry New Zealand, Lichen, The Pacific Review, Contemporary Rhyme, Barnwood Poetry Magazine* and *The Feathertale Review*, and in hundreds of others. Accompanying videos to some of his videos can be found on YouTube.

Steve Redwood, author of *Fisher of Devils*, was born on a rainy day in Britain a long long time ago. It was still raining twenty-five years later, so he left the country in a huff, a raincoat, and a plane. He is at present hiding out in Madrid.

Due to a cold-blooded mixture of bribes, threats, and tearful cover letters, Redwood has managed to get around fifty short stories published in various small press magazines, mainly genre but also literary and even feminist, under the name of a pig-rearing imaginary sister.

Rhys Hughes is one of the most prolific and successful authors in Wales, although his work has rarely been available in his own country. His earliest publications were chess problems and mathematical puzzles for newspapers.

Rhys's latest novels, *The Postmodern Mariner* and *The Less Lonely Planet,* are due out soon.

Deb Hoag has been writing professionally for nearly 20 years, starting at a weekly alternative newspaper in Detroit, Michigan, *The Metro Times.* Her work there included answering phones, editing, writing a column and organizing such events as the Detroit Music Awards and the newspaper's yearly photography contest and 'Best of' issues. In the early 90s, Deb went back to school and was awarded a PhD in clinical psychology at the University of Detroit-Mercy. Since embarking on her new career, Deb's worked on the White Mountain Apache Indian Reservation in a variety of mental health positions, and is currently the impatient therapist at the psychiatric hospital in Show Low, Arizona.

Micci Oaten is the singer/songwriter of the alternative rock band Paparazzi Whore. She also runs the studio where she produces, programmes and arranges all the songs. The band has a song in the Hollywood slasher movie *Red Hook* (October 2008). When Micci isn't working with the band, she is a photographic model. For more information including updates on gigs visit her Myspace at myspace.com/paparazziwhore

Kevin Brown recently won the *Permafrost Literary Journal*'s Midnight Sun Fiction Contest, the Touchstone Fiction Competition, and placed third in the Cadenza Fiction Contest. He was also nominated for the 2007 *Best American Short Stories* and a 2007 Journey Award, and has been published in *Space & Time*, *Alligator Juniper*, *sub-TERRAIN*, *Rosebud*, *New Delta Review*, *Outercast*, *Underground Voices*, *Shakespeare's Monkey*, *Vulcan*, *HeavyGlow*, and *NANO Fiction*.

John Horner Jacobs' story, 'Sneaking In', will be published in *Doorways Magazine*'s 2008 Fall Issue. He studied at the Bennington Writers Workshop with Dana Gioia and Arturo Vivante.

J. Michael Shell's fiction has appeared in *Tropic: The Sunday Magazine of the Miami Herald*, the '07 edition of *Southern Fried Weirdness*, *Bound For Evil*, *Twisted Tongue* and *Tabbard Inn*. He will also have fiction appearing in *The Subatomic Anthology* (June '08), *Sounds of the Night* (August '08), and *Ballista* (Sept. '08). He studied at the University of South Carolina (BA in English)..

Marshall Payne has 18 published stories of SF and fantasy and is an interviewer and reviewer for *The Fix*.

Garrett Cook is a twenty-five-year old author of surreal/cross-genre fiction. His novel *Murderland Part 1: H8* is coming in July from Evil Nerd Empire.

Janett L. Grady is a fictioneer who currently lives in Palmer, Alaska.

Robert Lamb received his BA in creative writing from the University of Tennessee and has worked as a high school teacher, journalist, newspaper editor and professional writer. He currently lives and works in Atlanta.

Janis Butler Holm has served as Associate Editor for *Wide Angle*, the film journal. Her essays, stories, poems, and performance pieces have appeared in small-press, national, and international magazines. *Jonesing for Samantha*, a one-act play, was produced at Manhattan Theatre Source last fall.

Michael R. Colangelo is a writer from Toronto.

Dave Migman is strange. Very strange. His debut novel, *The Wolf Stepped Out*, is released in 2009 by Dog Horn Publishing.

Frank Burton has been published in *Poetry Monthly, Etchings, Skive, Monkey Kettle, Twisted Tongue, The Beat* and *Whispers of Wickedness*. In 2009 his collection *A History of Sarcasm* is released by Dog Horn Publishing.

RC Edrington has been a scourge on the small press for years. His poetry and prose are an ever evolving, brutally honest autobiography. To read more please visit rcedrington.com.

Adam Lowe, AKA Beyoncé Holes, is a libertine, heretic and Editor-in-Chief at Dog Horn Publishing. He currently resides in a squat located on the boundary between at least three universes, and lives with a mango tree, an Egyptian deity (Amaunet) and a fallen angel called Dave. He keeps six lovers, a time-travelling pet dodo from the past and a constantly inebriated brain. He also edits *Polluto: The Anti-Pop Culture Journal*, is Features Editor for *Bent* and runs a clubnight called Blasphemy in his hometown of Leeds, UK. We're yet to verify any of this information

SUBMISSIONS

Issue 4: Queer and Loathing in Wonderland is out in winter, 2008. - Think about the body and gender; think about sex; think about the landscapes we live in, the ideals we strive for and the utopian dream; think about urban existence and disaffection; think about gonzo journalism and the collapse between fiction and non-fiction; think about weird places and strained interactions in a place full of strangers.

All submissions must have a countercultural element. By this we mean an enagagement with, challenging of or subverting of popular cultures and ideologies. Many submissions lack this important point. Remember: we are 'The Anti-Pop Culture Journal'. If you want to know what that means, read tthis copy and see how our mission statement and our themes come together. Read the editorial introduction. Read the stories. Read the poems. Look at the art. Read the columns. Then ask yourself, 'Can I really imagine myself alongside these works?' If you can, then submissions should be sent, as always, to editor@polluto.com.